George Washington

The proceedings of the Executive of the United States,

Respecting the insurgents, 1794

George Washington

The proceedings of the Executive of the United States,
Respecting the insurgents, 1794

ISBN/EAN: 9783337731236

Printed in Europe, USA, Canada, Australia, Japan

Cover: Foto ©ninafisch / pixelio.de

More available books at **www.hansebooks.com**

THE

PROCEEDINGS

OF THE

EXECUTIVE

OF THE

UNITED STATES,

RESPECTING

THE INSURGENTS.

1794.

PHILADELPHIA:

PRINTED BY JOHN FENNO,

PRINTER TO THE SENATE OF THE UNITED STATES.

M.DCC.XCV.

In Senate of the United States.

February 21ft, 1795.

ORDERED, That *five hundred copies of the papers hereafter enumerated, delivered with the meſſage of the Preſident of the United States, of 19th November laſt, be printed to wit :*

No. 1. *Judge Wilſon's certificate.*

    2. *The Proclamation of 7th Auguſt.*

    3. *The inſtruſtions of the Commmiſſioners.*

    4. *The report of the Commiſſioners.*

    5. *The Proclamation of 25th September.*

    6. *The correſpondence between the Governour of Pennſylvania and the Secretary for the department of State.*

    7. *The Report of the Secretary for the department of Treaſury to the Preſident of the United States.*

    8. *The Inſtruſtions to the Governour of Virginia.*

Atteſt,

SAMUEL A. OTIS, Secretary.

(No. 1.)

S i r,

FROM Evidence, which has been laid before me, I hereby notify to you, that, in the counties of Washington and Alleghany in Pennsylvania; Laws of the United States are opposed, and the Execution thereof obstructed by Combinations too powerful to be suppressed by the ordinary course of judicial Proceedings, or by the powers vested in the Marshal of that District.

I have the honour to be, with

The highest consideration and Respect,

Sir,

Your most obedient and

very humble servant

JAMES WILSON.

Philadelphia, 4th *August* 1794.

THE PRESIDENT of ⎱
the United States. ⎰

(True Copy)

GEO. TAYLOR, Jr.

(No. 2.)

By the PRESIDENT of the UNITED STATES of
AMERICA.

A PROCLAMATION.

WHEREAS combinations to defeat the execution of the
laws laying duties upon Spirits distilled within the
United States and upon Stills, have from the time of the commencement of those laws existed in some of the Western
parts of Pennsylvania. And Whereas the said Combinations,
proceeding in a manner subversive equally of the just authority
of Government and of the rights of individuals have hitherto
effected their dangerous and criminal purpose ; by the influence of certain irregular meetings whose proceedings have
tended to encourage and uphold the spirit of opposition, by
misrepresentations of the laws calculated to render them odious, by endeavours to deter those who might be so disposed
from accepting offices under them, through fear of public re-
sentment and of injury to person and property, and to compel
those who had accepted such offices by actual violence to surrender or forbear the execution of them ;—by circulating vindictive menaces against all those who should otherwise directly
or indirectly aid in the execution of the said laws, or who,
yielding to the dictates of conscience and to a sense of obligation should themselves comply therewith, by actually injuring
and destroying the property of persons who were understood
to have so complied ;—by inflicting cruel and humiliating
punishments upon private citizens for no other cause than
that of appearing to be the friends of the laws ;—by inter-
cepting the public officers on the high ways, abusing, assault-
ing and otherwise ill treating them ;—by going to their hou-

fes in the night, gaining admittance by force, taking away their papers and committing other outrages ; employing for thefe unwarrantable purpofes the agency of armed banditti, difguifed in fuch manner as for the moft part to efcape difcovery : And Whereas the endeavors of the Legiflature to obviate objections to the faid laws, by lowering the duties and by other alterations conducive to the convenience of thofe whom they immediately affect, (though they have given fatisfaction in other quarters) and the endeavors of the Executive Officers to conciliate a compliance with the laws, by explanations, by forbearance and even by particular accommodations fonnded on the fuggeftion of local confiderations, have been difappointed of their effect by the machinations of perfons whofe induftry to excite refiftance has increafed with every appearance of a difpofition among the people to relax in their oppofition and to acquiefce in the laws : Infomuch that many perfons in the faid Weftern parts of Pennfylvania have at length been hardy enough to perpetrate acts which I am advifed amount to treafon, being overt acts of levying war againft the United States ; the faid perfons having on the fixteenth and feventeenth of July laft paft proceded in arms (on the fecond day amonnting to feveral hundreds) to the houfe of John Neville, Infpector of the Revenue for the fourth Survey of the Diftrict of Pennfylvania, having repeatedly attacked the faid houfe with the perfons therein wounding fome of them ;—having feized David Lenox, Marfhal of the Diftrict of Pennfylvania, who previous thereto had been fired upon, while in the execution of his duty, by a party of armed men detaining him for fome time prifoner, till for the prefervation of his life and the obtaining of his liberty he found it neceffary to enter into ftipulations to forbear the execution of certain official duties touching proceffes iffuing out of a Court of the United States. And having finally obliged the faid Infpector of the Revenue and the faid Marfhal from confiderations of perfonal fafety to fly from that part of the Country, in order by a circuitous route to proceed to the Seat of Government ; avowing as the motives of thefe outrageous proceedings an intention to prevent by force of arms the execution of the faid laws, to oblige the faid Infpector of the Revenue to renounce his faid office, to withftand by open violence the lawful authority of the Government of the United States, and to compel thereby an alteration in the meafures of the Legiflature and a repeal of the laws aforefaid. And Whereas by a law of the United States, intitled " An Act to provide for calling forth the militia to execute the laws of the Union, fupprefs infurrections and repel invafions," it is enacted, " that whenever the laws of the United States fhall be oppofed or the execution thereof obftructed in any State by combinations too powerful to be fuppreffed by the ordinary courfe of judicial proceedings or by the powers vefted in the Marfhals by that act, the fame being notified by an affociate Juftice or the Diftrict Judge, it fhall be lawful for the Prefident of the United States to call forth the militia of fuch State to fupprefs fuch combinations and to caufe the laws to be duly executed. And if the militia of a State where fuch combinations may happen fhall refufe or be infufficient to fupprefs the fame it fhall be lawful for the Prefident if the Legiflature of the United States fhall not be in Seffion to call forth and employ fuch numbers of the militia of any other State or States moft convenient thereto, as may be neceffary, and the ufe of the militia fo to be called forth may be continued, if neceffary, until the expiration of thirty days after the commencement of the enfuing feffion : Provided always that whenever it may be neceffary in the judgment of the Prefident to ufe the military force hereby directed to be called forth ; The Prefident fhall forthwith and previous thereto,

by Proclamation, command such insurgents to disperse and retire peaceably to their respective abodes within a limited time."
And Whereas, James Wilson, an Associate Justice, on the
fourth instant by writing under his hand did, from evidence
which had been laid before him, notify to me that " in the
Counties of Washington and Alleghany in Pennsylvania laws
of the United States are opposed, and the execution thereof
obstructed by combinations too powerful to be suppressed by
the ordinary course of Judicial proceedings or by the powers
vested in the Marshal of that District." And Whereas it is
in my judgment, necessary under the circumstances of the
case, to take measures for calling forth the militia, in order
to suppress the Combinations aforesaid, and to cause the laws
to be duly executed—and, I have accordingly determined
so to do, feeling the deepest regret for the occasion, but
withal, the most solemn conviction, that the essential interests
of the Union demand it—that the very existence of Government, and the fundamental principles of social order, are
materially involved in the issue; and that the patriotism and
firmness of all good Citizens are seriously called upon, as occasion may require, to aid in the effectual suppression of so
fatal a spirit.

WHEREFORE, and in pursuance of the Proviso above recited, I George Washington, President of the United States,
do hereby command all persons, being Insurgents as aforesaid, and all others whom it may concern, on or before the first
day of September next, to disperse and retire peaceably to
their respective abodes. And I do moreover, warn all persons whomsoever, against aiding, abetting or comforting the
perpetrators of the aforesaid treasonable acts : And do require
all Officers and other Citizens, according to their respective

B

duties and the laws of the land, to exert their utmoft endeavors to prevent and fupprefs fuch dangerous proceedings.

In testimony whereof, I have caufed the Seal of the United States of America to be affixed to thefe Prefents, and figned the fame with my (L. S.) hand. Done at the City of Philadelphia the Seventh Day of Auguft, One Thoufand Seven Hundred and Ninety Four, and of the Independence of the United States of America, the Nineteenth.

Gº. WASHINGTON.

By the President.

EDM. RANDOLPH.

True Copy.

GEO. TAYLOR, Jr.

(No. 3.)

To James Ross, Jasper Yeates, William Bradford—

Gentlemen,

THE recent events in the neighborhood of Pittſburgh, have called the attention of the Preſident to the formation of ſome plan by which the inſurrection may be ſuppreſſed.

The intelligence which has been tranſmitted, having been laid before Judge Wilſon, he has granted a Certificate, declaring that the oppoſition to the laws of the United States, in the counties of Waſhington and Alleghany, cannot be ſuppreſſed, by the ordinary courſe of Judicial Proceedings, or the power of the Marſhal. A copy of that Certificate is encloſed (No. 1.)

You or any one or more of you are, therefore authorized and appointed forthwith, to proceed to the ſcene of the inſurrection and to confer with any bodies of men or individuals with whom you ſhall think proper to confer, in order to quiet and extinguiſh it. There is reaſon to believe that a collection of diſcontented individuals, will be found at Mingo Creek on the fourteenth inſtant, and as the object of their aſſembling, is undoubtedly to concert meaſures relative to this very ſubject, it is indiſpenſably neceſſary, that you ſhould preſs thither with the utmoſt expedition, It is uncertain whether they will remain together for a long or ſhort time— therefore the being on the ground on the day firſt named for their meeting is neceſſary to prevent a miſcarriage.

Theſe are the outlines of your communication—

1ſt. To ſtate the ſerious impreſſions which their conduct has created in the mind of the Executive, and to dilate upon.

the dangers attending every Government where laws are obstructed in their execution.

2d. To inform them that the evidence of the late transactions has been submitted to a Judge of the Supreme Court, and that he has granted the above mentioned Certificate whence a power has arisen to the President to call out the Militia to suppress the insurrection (see the Act of May 2d, 1792.)

3d. To represent to them, how painful an idea it is, to exercise such a power, and that it is the earnest wish of the President, to render it unnecessary by those endeavors which humanity, a love of peace and tranquility, and the happiness of his fellow-citizens, dictate.

4th. You will then explain your appointment as Commissioners in a language and with sentiments most conciliatory, but reconcileable to the self-respect which this Government ought to observe.

5th. Whether you are to proceed further, and in what manner must depend upon your judgment and discretion at the moment, after an estimate of the characters with whom you are conversing, their views, their influence, &c. &c.

6th. Whensoever you shall come to the point at which it may be necessary to be explicit, you are to declare that with respect to the excise-law, the President is bound to consider it, as much among the laws which he is to see executed, as any other. That as to the repeal of it, he cannot undertake to make any stipulation, that being a subject consigned by the Constitution to the Legislature from whom alone a change of legislative measures can be obtained. That he is willing to grant an amnesty and perpetual oblivion for every thing which has past—and cannot doubt, that any penalty to which the late tranfactions may have given birth, under the laws and within the jurifdiction of Pennfylvania may be alfo wiped away—but upon the following conditions—

·That fatisfactory affurances be given that the laws be no longer obftructed in their execution by any combinations directly or indirectly, and that the Offenders againft whom procefs fhall iffue for a violation of, or an oppofition·to, the laws fhall not be protected from the free operation of the law. —Nothing will be enforced concerning the duties of former years, if they will fairly comply for the prefent year.

7th. If they fpeak of the hardfhip of being drawn to the federal Courts at a diftance, to that no other reply can be made than this—that the inconvenience whatfoever it may be, was the act of their own Reprefentatives, and is continued as being ftill their fenfe—that however on all occafions which will permit the State Courts to be ufed without inconvenience to the United States or danger of their being fruftrated in the object of the fuits and profecutions the State Courts will be reforted to—but the choice of jurifdictions muft always depend upon the difcretion of the United States, and therefore nothing more fpecific can be faid at prefent.

8th. Whenfoever you fhall choofe to fpeak of the ulterior meafures of the Government, you will fay that orders have already iffued for the proper Militia to hold themfelves in readinefs, and that every thing is prepared for their movement, as will be feen by the Proclamation (No. 3), and is known to yourfelves from the communications of the Government; but that thefe movements will be fufpended until your return.

9th. Thefe are faid to be the *outlines*—You will fill them up and modify them fo as moft effectually to prevent if poffible, the laſt dreadful neceſſity which the Preſident ſo much, deprecates, and you may in particular aſſure any individuals of pardon who will expiate their offence by a compliance with the law.

10th. You will keep the Executive minutely and conſtantly informed of all your proceedings and will uſe Expreſſes whenſoever you think proper at the public expenſe.

11th. You will be allowed eight dollars per day, and your expenſes, and may employ a proper perſon to act as your Clerk, who ſhall be paid whatſoever you may certify him to deſerve. The ſum of one thouſand dollars is advanced to you on account.

12th. William Bradford is empowered to add the name of Thomas Smith, or any other proper perſon, if either J. Roſs or J. Yeates ſhall refuſe or be unable to attend.

EDM. RANDOLPH,
Sec'y of State.

5th Auguſt, 1794.

DEPARTMENT of STATE,

Auguſt 8th, 1794.

To James Ross, Jasper Yeates, William Bradford—

Gentlemen,

In purſuance of Inſtructions from the Preſident of the United States, you or any one or more of you, are hereby authorized and empowered forthwith to repair to the Counties on the Weſtern ſide of the Alleghany mountain in the State of Pennſylvania, there to confer with ſuch bodies or individuals, as you may approve concerning the commotions, which are referred to in the Proclamation of the Prefident of the United States, bearing date the 7th day of Auguft inftant —and whatfoever promife or engagement you fhall make in behalf of the Executive of the United States, the fame will be ratified in the moft ample manner.

(L. S.) GIVEN under my Hand and the Seal of Office of the Department of State, the Eighth day of Auguft 1794.

EDM. RANDOLPH,
Secretary of State.

(True Copy)

GEO. TAYLOR, Jr.

(No. 4.)

The COMMISSIONERS, *appointed to confer with the Citizens in the Weſtern Counties of Pennſylvania, in order to induce them to ſubmit peaceably to the laws, and to prevent the neceſſity of uſing coercion to inforce their execution, reſpectfully Report to the Preſident of the United States*

THAT in purſuance of their inſtructions, they repaired to the weſtern counties; and, on their arrival there, found that the ſpirit of diſaffection had pervaded other parts of the fourth ſurvey of Pennſylvania, beſides thoſe counties declared to be in a ſtate of inſurrection;—that all the offices of inſpection eſtabliſhed therein had lately been violently ſuppreſſed,—and that a meeting of perſons, choſen by moſt of the townſhips, was aſſembled at Parkinſon's ferry, for the purpoſe of taking into conſideration the ſituation of the weſtern country. This aſſembly, compoſed of citizens coming from every part of the fourth ſurvey, would have furniſhed a favourable opportunity for a conference and mutual explanation; but as they met in the open fields, and were expoſed to the impreſſions of a number of raſh and violent men (ſome of them armed) who ſurrounded them, an immediate communication with the whole body would have been inconvenient and hazardous. The meeting was probably of that opinion alſo; for ſoon after the appointment of Commiſſioners was announced to them, they reſolved that a Committee, to conſiſt of three perſons from each county, ſhould be appointed to meet any commiſſioners that might have been, or might be appointed by the government; and that they ſhould report the reſult of their conference to the ſtanding Committee, which was to be compoſed of one perſon from each townſhip. As ſoon as this Committee of conference were nominated, they agreed to meet at Pittſburg on the 20th of the ſame month.

The underwritten accordingly repaired to that place, and were ſoon after joined by the honorable Thomas M'Kean and William Irvine, Eſquires, who had been appointed Commiſſioners on the part of the Executive of Pennſylvania. A full and free communication was immediately had with thoſe gentlemen as to the powers delegated, and the meaſures proper to be purſued at the expected conference.

On the day appointed, a ſub-committee of the Conferees waited on the Commiſſioners, and arranged with them the time, place and manner of Conference. It was agreed, that it ſhould be had the next morning, at the houſe of John M'Maſters, in Pittſburg, and ſhould be private.

On the 21ſt, all the Commiſſioners met the Conferees, at the place appointed. Of the latter there were preſent, John Kirkpatrick, George Smith, and John Powers, from Weſt-moreland county; David Bradford, James Marſhall, and James Edgar, from Waſhington county; Edward Cook, Albert Gallatin, and James Lang, from Fayette county; Thomas Morton, John Lucas, H. H. Brackenridge, from Alleghany county; together with William M'Kinley, William Suther-land, and Robert Stevenſon, who were inhabitants of Ohio county, in Virginia.

The conference was begun by the underwritten, who ex-preſſed the concern they felt at the events, which had occa-ſioned that meeting; but declared their intention to avoid any unneceſſary obſervations upon them, ſince it was their buſineſs to endeavour to compoſe the diſturbances which pre-vailed, and to reſtore the authority of the laws, by meaſures wholly of a conciliatory nature.

C

It was then ſtated, that the formal reſiſtance which had lately been given to the laws of the United States, violated the great principle on which republican government is founded ; that every ſuch government muſt, at all hazards, enforce obedience to the general will ; and that ſo long as they admitted themſelves to be a part of the nation, it was manifeſtly abſurd to oppoſe the national authority.

The underwritten then proceeded to ſtate the obligations which lay on the Preſident of the United States to cauſe the laws to be executed ;—the meaſures he had taken for that purpoſe ;—his deſire to avoid the neceſſity of coercion ;— and the general nature of the powers he had veſted in them ; and finally, requeſted to know, Whether the conferees could give any aſſurances of a diſpoſition in the people to ſubmit to the laws, or would recommend ſuch ſubmiſſion to them ?

The Commiſſioners on the part of the State of Pennſylvania, then addreſſed the Conferees, on the ſubject of the late diſturbances in that country ; forcibly repreſented the miſchievous conſequences of ſuch conduct ; explained the nature of their miſſion ; and declared, they were ready to promiſe in behalf of the Executive authority of the ſtate a full pardon and indemnity, for all that was paſt, on condition of an entire ſubmiſſion to the laws.

On the part of the Conferees, a narrative was given of thoſe cauſes of diſcontent and uneaſineſs which very generally prevailed in the minds of the people, in the weſtern counties, and which had diſcovered themſelves in the late tranſactions. Many of theſe, they ſaid, had long exiſted, and ſome of them from the ſettlement of that country. Among other cauſes of diſcontent, they complained of the deciſions of the State Courts, which diſcountenanced improvement-titles, and gave the preference to paper-titles ;—of the war which had ſo long vexed the frontiers—and of the manner in which that war had been conducted. They complained, that they

had been continually harraſſed by militia duty, in being called out by the State Government, to repel incurſions, &c.—
that the General Government had been inattentive to the
execution of the Treaty of Peace, reſpecting the Weſtern
Poſts, and remiſs in aſſerting the claim to the navigation of
the Miſſiſippi ;—that the acts for raiſing a revenue on Diſtilled Spirits were unequal and oppreſſive, in conſequence of
their local circumſtances ;—that Congreſs had neglected their
remonſtrances and petitions ; and that there was great hard-
ſhip in being ſummoned to anſwer for penalties in the Courts
of the United States at a diſtance from the vicinage. They
alſo mentioned the ſuſpenſion of the ſettlement at Preſqu'iſle ;
the engroſſing of large quantities of land in the State by individuals ;—the killing of certain perſons at General Neville's
houſe ; and the ſending of ſoldiers from the garriſon at Pittsburg, to defend his houſe—as cauſes of irritation among the
people. To theſe they added the appointment of General
Neville, as Inſpector of the Survey, whoſe former popula-
rity had made his acceptance of that office particularly offen-
ſive.

They ſaid, they were perſuaded, that the perſons who were
the actors in the late diſturbances, had not originally intended to have gone ſo far as they had gone ; but were led to it
from the obſtinacy of thoſe who refuſed to do what was demanded of them ; that the forcible oppoſition which had been
made to the law, was owing to the preſſure of the grievance ;
but, if there was any proſpect of redreſs, no people would
be more ready to ſhow themſelves good citizens.

The Commiſſioners expreſſed their ſurprize at the extent
of theſe complaints, and intimated, that if all theſe matters
were really cauſes of uneaſineſs and diſſatisfaction in the minds
of the people, it would be impoſſible for any government to
ſatisfy them. But as ſome of theſe complaints were of a nature more ſerious than others, though they could not ſpeak

officially, they ftated what was generally underftood as to the conduct, meafures, and expectations of government refpecting the Miffifippi navigation ; the treaty of peace ; the fufpenfion of the fettlement at Prefqu'ifle, &c.—that as to the acts of Congrefs, which had been forcibly oppofed, if it were proper they fhould be repealed, Congrefs alone could do it ; but that while they *were* laws, they muft be carried into execution ;—that the petitions of the weftern counties had not been neglected, nor their interefts overlooked ;—that in fact the local interefts of thofe counties were better reprefented than thofe of any other part of the State ; they having no lefs than three gentlemen in the Houfe of Reprefentatives, when it appeared by the cenfus, that their numbers would not entitle them to two ;—that the acts in queftion had been often under the confideration of Congrefs ; that they had always been fupported by a confiderable majority, in which they would find the names of feveral gentlemen, confidered, in thofe counties, as the firmeft friends of their country ;—that although the general interefts of the union did not admit of a repeal, modifications had been made in the law, and fome favourable alterations, in confequence of their reprefentations ; and, that at the laft feffion, the ftate courts had been vefted with a jurifdiction over offences againft thofe acts, which would enable the Prefident to remove one of their principal complaints ;—that the convenience of the people had been, and would always be confulted by the government ;—and the Conferees were defired to fay, if there was any thing in the power of the Executive, that yet remained to be done to make the execution of the acts convenient and agreeable to the people.

One of the Conferees then enquired, whether the Prefident could not fufpend the execution of the excife acts, until the meeting of Congrefs ; but he was interrupted by others, who declared that they confidered fuch a meafure as impracticable. The Commiffioners expreffed the fame opinion ; and the converfation then became more particular, refpecting the powers the Commiffioners poffeffed; the propriety and neceffity of the Conferees expreffing their fenfe, upon the propofals to be made, and of their calling the ftanding Committee together, before the 1ft September. But as it was agreed, that the propofitions and anfwers fhould be reduced to writing, the refult is contained in the documents annexed, and it appears unneceffary to detail the conference further.

The underwritten accordingly prefented to the Conferees a letter, of which a copy, marked No. 1, is annexed : and the following day they received an anfwer from them, in which they declare ; that, they are fatisfied, that the Executive had in its propofals gone as far as could be expected; that in their opinion, it was the intereft of the country to accede to the law; and that they would endeavour to conciliate not only the Committee, to whom they were to report, but the public mind in general, to their fenfe of the fubject. A copy of this letter alfo is annexed, No. 2,

The underwritten then proceeded to ftate in writing what affurances of fubmiffion would be deemed full and fatisfactory, and to detail more particularly the engagements they had power to make. This detail was fubmitted to the infpection of a fub-committee of the Conferees, who candidly fuggefted fuch alterations as appeared to them neceffary to render the propofals acceptable. From a defire to accommodate, moft of the alterations fuggefted by thofe gentlemen, were adopted ; and though fome of them were rejected, the reafons given appeared to be fatisfactory, and no further objections remained. A copy of this detail is marked No. 3.

The Conferees, on the following day, explicitly approved of the detail thus fettled, engaged to recommend the propofals to the people, and added, that however it might be received, they were perfuaded nothing more could be done by the Commiffioners, or them, to bring the bufinefs to an accommodation. No. 4, is a copy of their letter.

So far as this letter refpects the gentlemen from Ohio county, in Virginia, a reply was made and fome arrangements entered into with them, the nature and extent of which appear, by the correfpondence; copies of which are annexed, numbered 5, 6, 7, and 8.

The hopes excited by the favourable iffue of this conference, were not realized by a correfpondent conduct in the citizens, who compofed what was called, 'the ftanding Committee.' They affembled at Brownfville (Redftone Old-Fort) on the 28th Auguft, and broke up on the 29th, and, on the following day a letter was received from Edward Cook, their chairman, announcing, that difficulties had arifen, and that a new Committee of conference was appointed : and, although the refolve which is annexed was paffed, it did not appear that the affurances of fubmiffion, which had been demanded, had been given. Copies of this letter and refolve, are marked No. 9 and 10.

The underwritten were informed by feveral of the members of that meeting, as well as other citizens who were prefent at it, that the report of the Committee of conference, and the propofals of the Commiffioners were unfavourably received; that rebellion and hoftile refiftance againft the United States were publicly recommended by fome of the members; and that fo exceffive a fpirit prevailed, that it was not thought prudent or fafe to urge a compliance with the terms and preliminaries, prefcribed by the underwritten, or the Commiffioners from the Governor of Pennfylvania. All that could be obtained was the refolve already mentioned, the queftion upon it being decided by *ballot*; by which means each member had an opportunity of concealing his opinion and of fheltering himfelf from the refentment of thofe from whom violence was apprehended. But notwithftanding this caution, the opinion was fo far from being unanimous, that out of fifty-feven votes, there were twenty-three nays, leaving a majority of only eleven : and the underwritten have been repeatedly affured, by differ nt members of that meeting, that if the queftion had been publicly put, it would have been carried in the negative, by a confiderable majority.

With a view of counteracting the arts and influence of the violent, the underwritten, on the 27th Auguft, addreffed a letter to the late Conferees, authorizing them to affure the friends of order, who might be difpofed to exert themfelves to reftore the authority of the laws, that they might rely on the protection of Government, and that meafures would be taken to fupprefs and punifh the violence of thofe individuals, who might diffent from the general fentiment. This letter (a copy of which is marked No. 11) was delivered to one of the Conferees going to Brownfville ; but he afterwards informed the underwritten, that the gentlemen to whom it was addreffed, did not ' think it prudent to make any ufe of it, as the temper, which prevailed was fuch that it would probably have done more harm than good.'

The conduct of the meeting at Brownfville, notwithftanding the thin veil thrown over it by the refolve already mentioned, was faid to be confidered by many, and efpecially by the violent party, as a rejection of the terms. It was certainly a partial rejection of thofe propofed by the underwritten, and a total one of the preliminaries prefcribed by the State Commiffioners, who had required affurances from the members of that meeting only, and not from the people themfelves.

Having therefore no longer any hopes of an univerfal or even general fubmiffion, it was deemed neceffary by a folemn appeal to the people, to afcertain as clearly as poffible the determination of every individual—to encourage and oblige the friends of order to declare themfelves—to recal as many of the difaffected as poffible, to their duty, by affurances of pardon dependant on their individual conduct—and to learn with certainty what oppofition government might expect if military coercion fhould be finally unavoidable.

To fecure thefe advantages, the underwritten were of opinion, that the affurances of fubmiffion required of the people ought not only to be publicly given, but ought alfo to be reduced to writing: and that the ftate of each County fhould be certified by thofe who were to fuperintend the meetings at which the difpofition of the people was to be afcertained.

On the firft inftant, nine of the gentlemen appointed by the meeting at Brownfville, affembled at Pittfburg, and in the afternoon requefted a conference with the Commiffioners, which was agreed to. They produced the refolves by which they were appointed and entered into fome explanation of the nature of their vifit: but being defired to communicate it in writing they withdrew, and foon after fent a letter addreffed to the Commiffioners of the United States, and of the ftate of Pennfylvania; to which an anfwer was immediately written. Copies of thefe letters are annexed, No. 12 and 13.

As no part of their letter, although addreffed to the Commiffioners from Pennfylvania, related to the preliminaries prefcribed by them, they made no anfwer in writing: but in a conference held the next morning with thofe nine gentlemen they verbally declared to them their entire concurrence in the fentiments contained in the letter from the underwritten; and they expreffed, at fome length, their furprize and regret at the conduct of the meeting at Brownfville. The Conferees declared themfelves fatisfied with the anfwer they had received—avowed an entire conviction of the neceffity and propriety of an early fubmiffion, in the manner propofed —and offered immediately to enter into the detail for fettling the time, place, and manner of taking the fenfe of the people. A copy of their letter, which alfo expreffes thefe fentiments, is annexed, No. 14.

It was accordingly agreed between the Commiffioners on the one part, and thefe gentlemen on the other, that the people fhould affemble for the purpofe of expreffing their determination, and giving the affurances required, on the 11th inft. ; and the mode of afcertaining the public fentiments of the citizens refident in the fourth furvey of Pennfylvania, was clearly and definitely prefcribed by the unanimous confent of all who were prefent at the conference. It was evident, that circumftances might arife to prevent the real difpofition of the citizens from being fully afcertained at thefe meetings, and that even arts might be ufed to procure fuch an expreffion of the public mind, that while it held up an appearance of fubmiffion, might be in reality a falfe and delufive reprefentation of it. It was therefore neceffary that perfons of character, from every townfhip or diftrict (who might be able from their own knowledge or the comparifon of all circumftances, juftly to appreciate the public opinion) fhould affemble and jointly certify their opinion whether there was fuch a general fubmiffion in their refpective counties, or not, that the laws could be peaceably carried into execution. For the fame purpofe it was agreed to be proper that the number of thofe who openly refufed, as well as of thofe who promifed to fubmit, in their refpective townfhips or diftricts, fhould be reported to the Commiffioners. A copy of this agreement, marked No. 15, is annexed.

It appears that meetings were held in the feveral counties

D

in purſuance of this agreement; but the underwritten, with extreme regret, find themſelves obliged to report, that in the returns made to them no opinions are certified that there is ſo general a ſubmiſſion in any one of the counties that an office of inſpection can be immediately and ſafely eſtabliſhed therein: on the contrary, the report of thoſe who ſuperintended the meeting in Weſtmoreland, ſtates their opinion to be that ſuch a meaſure would not be ſafe.

From Alleghany county no report whatever has been received, and although it is underſtood that a very great majority of thoſe aſſembled in the Pittſburgh diſtrict, actually ſubſcribed the declarations required, yet there is no reaſon to believe that there was a favorable iſſue in any other diſtrict. Information has been received that great violence prevailed in one of them, and that in another the majority declared their determination not to ſubmit to the laws of the United States.

From Waſhington county a general return was duly tranſmitted to one of the Commiſſioners at Union Town, ſigned by twenty-eight of the ſuperintendants of the meeting: they do not however ſtate the number of the yeas and nays on the queſtion for ſubmiſſion; they decline giving any opinion whether there is ſuch a general ſubmiſſion that an office of inſpection may be eſtabliſhed therein, but certify their opinion and belief, " that a large majority of the inhabitants will " acquieſce and ſubmit to the ſaid law, under a hope and " firm belief that the Congreſs of the United States will re- " peal the law."

The report from the Superintendants in Weſtmoreland county is equally defective, in not ſtating the numbers as required; but it certifies their opinion that as ill diſpoſed, lawleſs perſons could ſuddenly aſſemble and offer violence, it would not be safe immediately to establish an office of inspection in that county.

The county of Fayette, rejected the mode of ascertaining the sense of the people which had been settled between the underwritten and the last Committee of conference at Pittsburgh. The standing Committee of that county directed those qualified by the laws of the state for voting at elections, to assemble in their election districts and vote by ballot, whether they would accede to the proposals made by the Commissioners of the United States, on the 22d of August, or not. The Superintendants of these election districts report, that five hundred and sixty of the people thus convened, had voted for submission, and that one hundred and sixty one had voted against it;—that no judge or member of their Committee had attended from the fourth district of the county, to report the state of the votes there, and that they are of opinion that a great majority of the citizens who did not attend, are disposed to behave peaceably and with due submission to the laws. But it is proper to mention, that credible and certain information has been received, that in the fourth district of that county (composed of the townships of Tyrone and Bullskin) of which the standing Committee have given no account, six sevenths of those who voted, were for resistance. Copies of the reports stated, are annexed, and numbered 16, 17, 18.

From that part of Bedford county which is comprehended within the fourth survey of Pennsylvania, no report or returns have been sent forward, nor has any information been received that the citizens assembled there for the purpose of declaring their opinions upon questions proposed.

The written assurances of submission which has been received by the Commissioners, are not numerous, nor were they given by all those who expressed a willingness to obey the laws. In Fayette county a different plan being purfued, no written affurances were given in the manner required. In the three other counties, which from the cenfus taken under the laws of the ftate, appear to contain above eleven thoufand taxable inhabitants (in which none under the age of twenty-one are included) the names fubfcribed to the papers received, barely exceed two thoufand feven hundred, and of thefe a very confiderable part have not been fubfcribed in the mode agreed on ; being either figned at a different day,—unattefted by any perfon,—or wilfully varied from the fettled form.

From credible information received, it appears to the under-written that in fome townfhips the majority, and in one of them the whole of the perfons affembled, publicly declared themfelves for refiftance : in fome, although the fenfe of the majority was not known, yet the party for refiftance was fuf-ficiently ftrong to prevent any declarations of fubmiffion being openly made ; and in others, the majority were intimi-dated or oppofed by a violent minority. But notwithftanding thefe circumftances, the underwritten firmly believe that there is a confiderable majority of the inhabitants of the fourth furvey, who are now difpofed to fubmit to the execution of the laws : at the fame time, they conceive it their duty expli-citly to declare their opinion, that fuch is the ftate of things in that furvey, that there is no probability that the act for raifing a revenue on diftilled fpirits and ftills, can at prefent be enforced by the ufual courfe of civil authority, and that fome more competent force is neceffary to caufe the laws to be duly executed, and to infure to the officers and well dif-pofed citizens that protection which it is the duty of govern-ment to afford.

This opinion is founded on the facts already ftated ; and it is confirmed by that which is entertained by many intelligent and influential perfons, officers of juftice and others, refiden in the weſtern counties, who have lately informed one of tho commiſſioners, that whatever aſſurances might be given, it was in their judgment abſolutely neceſſary that the civil authority ſhould be aided by a military force, in order to ſecure a due execution of the laws.

JAMES ROSS,
J. YEATES,
WM. BRADFORD,

Philadelphia, Sept. 24, 1794.

The Documents referred to in the aforegoing Report.

(No. 1.)

From the Commiſſioners on the part of the Union, to the Committee of Conference, aſſembled at Pittſburgh.

Pittſburgh, Auguſt 21, 1794.

GENTLEMEN,

HAVING had a conference with you on the important ſubjeƈt that calls us into this part of Pennſylvania, we ſhall now ſtate to you in writing, agreeably to your requeſt, the nature and objeƈt of our miſſion hither. Conſidering this as a criſis infinitely intereſting to our fellow-citizens who have authoriſed you to confer with us, we ſhall explain ourſelves to you with that franknefs and ſincerity, which the ſolemnity of the occaſion demands.

You well know that the Preſident of the United States is charged with the execution of the laws. Obedience to the national will being indiſpenſable in a republican government, the people of the United States have ſtrictly enjoined it as his duty "to ſee that the laws are faithfully executed :"—and when the ordinary authorities of the government are incompetent for that end, he is bound to exert thoſe high powers with which the nation has inveſted him for ſo extraordinary an occaſion.

It is but too evident that the inſurrections which have lately prevailed in ſome of theſe weſtern counties have ſuppreſſed the uſual exerciſe of the civil authority ; and it has been formally notified to the Preſident, by one of the Aſſociate Judges, in the manner the law preſcribes, "that in the counties of Waſhington and Alleghany, in Pennſylvania, laws of the United States are oppoſed, and the execution thereof obſtructed by combinations too powerful to be ſuppreſſed by the ordinary courſe of judicial proceedings, or the powers veſted in the Marſhal of that Diſtrict." He therefore perceives, with the deepeſt regret, the neceſſity to which he may be reduced, of calling forth the national force in order to ſupport the national authority, and to cauſe the laws to be executed ;—but he has determined, previouſly, to addreſs himſelf to the patriotiſm and reaſon of the people of the weſtern counties, and to try the moderation of government, in hopes that he may not be compelled to reſort to its ſtrength. But, we muſt not conceal from you, that it is alſo his fixed determination, if theſe hopes ſhould be diſappointed, to employ the force,—and if it be neceſſary, the whole force of the Union, to ſecure the execution of the laws. He has, therefore, authoriſed us to repair hither, and by free conferences and the powers veſted in us, to endeavor to put an end to the preſent diſturbances, and to the oppoſition to the execution of the laws, in a manner that may be finally ſatisfactory to all our fellow-citizens.

We hope that this moderation in the government will not be mifconftrued by the citizens to whom we are fent. The Prefident, who feels a paternal folicitude for their welfare, wifhes to prevent the calamities that are impending over them—to ftate to them clearly the inevitable confequences of further refiftance—to recall them to their duty—and to prove to the whole world, that if military coercion muft be employed, it is *their* choice and not *his.*

The powers vefted in us, will enable us fo to arrange the execution of the acts for raifing a revenue on diftilled fpirits and ftills, that little inconvenience will arife therefrom to the people—to prevent as far as is confiftent with the public interefts the commencing profecutions under thofe acts at a diftance from the places where the delinquents refide—to fufpend profecutions for the late offences againft the United States—and, even, to engage for a general pardon and oblivion of them.

But, gentlemen, we explicitly declare to you, that the exercife of thefe powers muft be preceded by full and fatisfactory affurances of a fincere determination in the people to obey the laws of the United States, and their eventual operation muft depend upon a correfpondent acquiefcence in the execution of the acts which have been oppofed. We have not, and coming from the Executive, you well know that we cannot have, any authority to fufpend the laws, or to offer the moft diftant hopes, that the acts, the execution of which has been obftructed, will be repealed. On the contrary, we are free to declare to you our private opinions, that the national councils, while they confult the general interefts of the republic, and endeavor to conciliate every part by local accomodations to citizens who refpect the laws, will fternly refufe every indulgence to men who accompany their requefts with threats, and refift by force the public authority.

Upon thefe principles, we are ready to enter with you into the detail neceffary for the exercife of our powers—to learn what local accommodations are yet wanting to render the execution of the laws convenient to the people—to concert with you meafures for reftoring harmony and order, and for burying the paft in oblivion ; and to unite our endeavors with your's to fecure the peace and happinefs of our common country.

It is neceffary, however, to apprife you thus early, that at prefent, we do not confider ourfelves as authorifed to enter into any conferences on this fubject, after the firft of September enfuing. We therefore hope the bufinefs will be fo conducted that fome definitive anfwer may be given to us before that day.

We cannot believe, that in fo great a crifis, any attempts to temporife and procraftinate will be made by thofe who fincerely love their country, and wifh to fecure its tranquility.

We alfo declare to you, that no indulgence will be given to any future offence againft the United States, and that they who fhall hereafter directly or indirectly oppofe the execution of the laws, muft abide the confequences of their conduct.

JAMES ROSS,
J. YEATES,
Wm. BRADFORD,.

(No. 2.)

The following is the answer of the Committee.

Pittsburg, Aug. 22, 1794.

GENTLEMEN,

HAVING in our conference, at confiderable length ftated to you the grounds of that difcontent which exifts in the minds of the people of this country, and which has lately fhewn itfelf in acts of oppofition to the Excife law, you will confider us as waving any queftion with regard to the nature of thofe acts, whether, reafonable, or amounting only to riot and breach of the peace; of courfe as waving the queftion of the conftitutional power of the Prefident to call upon the force of the union to fupprefs them. It is our object, as it is yours, to compofe the difturbance.

We are fatisfied that in fubftance, you have gone as far as we could expect the Executive to go. It only remains to afcertain your propofitions more in detail, and to fay, what arrangements it may be in your power to make with regard to convenience in collecting the revenue under the Excife laws,—how far it may be confiftent with the public intereft to prevent commencing profecutions under thofe laws at a diftance from the places where the delinquents refide,—on what condition or circumftance profecutions for the late violations of the laws fhall be fufpended; that is to fay, whether on the individual keeping the peace, or on its being kept by the country in general,—and alfo with regard to the general amnefty, whether the claiming the benefit of it by an individual fhall depend on his own future conduct or that of the whole community.

We have already ftated to you in conference that we are empowered to give you no definitive anfwer with regard to the fenfe of the people on the great queftion of acceding to the law; but that in our opinion, it is the intereft of the country to accede; and that we fhall make this report to the Committee to whom we

E

are to report, and ftate to them the reafons of our opinion, that fo far as they may appear to have weight they may be regarded by them. It will be our endeavor to conciliate, not only them, but the public mind in general to our fenfe on this fubject : for this purpofe we hope to be affifted by you in giving all that extent and precifion, clearnefs and certainty to your propofitions as may fatisfy the underftandings and engage the acquiefcence of the people.

It is to be underftood that in acceding to the law, no inference is to be drawn, or conftruction made that we will relinquifh a conftitutional oppofition ; but that we will invariably, undeviatingly and conftantly purfue every legal means and meafure of obtaining a repeal of the law in queftion.

As we are difpofed with you to have the fenfe of the people taken on the fubject of our conference as fpeedily as may be, with that view we have refolved to call the Committee to whom our report is to be made, at an earlier day than had been appointed, to wit, to meet on Thurfday the 28th inft. but have not thought ourfelves juftifiable in changing the place, to wit, at Redftone (Old Fort) on the Monongahela.

By order of the Committee,

EDWARD COOK, *Chairman.*

To the Commiffioners on }
the part of the Union. }

(No. 3.)

THE Commiffioners appointed by the Prefident of the United States, to confer with the citizens in the weftern parts of Pennfylvania, having been affured by the Committee of conference, of their determination to approve the propofals made, and to recommend to the general Committee appointed by the meeting at Parkinfon's ferry, a fubmiffion to the acts of Congrefs, do now proceed to declare what affurances of fubmiffion will be deemed full and fatisfactory, and to detail the engagements which they have power to make.

1. It is expected and required by the faid Commiffioners, that

the citizens compoſing the ſaid general Committee, do on or be.
fore the firſt day of September, explicitly declare their determination to ſubmit to the laws of the United States, and that they
will not directly or indirectly oppoſe the execution of the acts for
raiſing a revenue on diſtilled ſpirits and ſtills.

2. That they do explicitly recommend a perfect and entire acquieſcence under the execution of the ſaid acts.

3. That they do in like manner recommend that no violence,
injuries or threats, be offered to the perſon or againſt the property
of any officer of the United States, or citizens complying with
the laws, and do declare their determination to ſupport (as far as
the laws require) the civil authority, in affording the protection
due to all officers and citizens.

4. That meaſures be taken to aſcertain by meetings in election
diſtricts or otherwiſe, the determination of the citizens in the
fourth ſurvey of Pennſylvania, to ſubmit to the ſaid laws ; and
that ſatisfactory aſſurances be given to the ſaid Commiſſioners
that the people have ſo determined to ſubmit, on or before the
14th of September next.

The ſaid Commiſſioners, if a full and perfect compliance with
the above requiſitions ſhall take place, have power to promiſe and
engage in manner following, to wit.

1. No proſecution for any treaſon or other indictable offence
againſt the United States, committed in the fourth ſurvey of
Pennſylvania before this day, ſhall be commenced or proceeded
on until the tenth of July next.

2. If there ſhall be a general and ſincere acquieſcence in the
execution of the ſaid laws, until the ſaid tenth day of July next,
a general pardon and oblivion of all ſuch offences ſhall be granted :
excepting therefrom, nevertheleſs, every perſon who ſhall in the
mean time wilfully obſtruct, or attempt to obſtruct the execution
of any of the laws of the United States, or be in any wiſe aiding
or abetting therein.

3. Congrefs having by an act paffed on the fifth day of June laft, authorifed the ftate courts to take cognizance of offences againft the faid acts for raifing a revenue upon diftilled fpirits and ftills, the Prefident has determined that he will direct fuits againft fuch delinquents to be profecuted therein ; if upon experiment it be found that local prejudices or other caufes do not obftruct the faithful adminiftration of juftice : But it is to be underftood, that of this he muft be the judge, and that he does not mean by this determination to impair any power vefted in the Executive of the United States.

4. Certain beneficial arrangements for adjufting delinquencies and profecutions for penalties now depending, fhall be made and communicated by the officers appointed to carry the faid acts into execution.

Given under our hands at Pittfburg, this 22d day of Auguft 1794.

> JAMES ROSS,
> J. YEATES,
> Wm. BRADFORD.

To the Committee }
of Conference. }

———

(No. 4.)

Pittfburg, Auguft 23, 1794.

Gentlemen,

WE prefume it has been underftood by you that the conference on our part confifts of members not only from the counties of Pennfylvania weft of the Allegheney mountains, but alfo from Ohio county, in Virginia, and your propofitions made in general by your firft letter being addreffed to this conference, the Ohio county was confidered as included ; yet in your propofitions made in detail by your laft, you confine them to the furvey within Pennfylvania. We would requeft an explanation on this particular.

We have only farther to fay, we fhall make a faithful report of your propofitions, which we approve of, and will recommend to the people, and however they may be received we are per-funded nothing more could have been done by you or us to bring this businefs to an accommodation.

Signed by order of the Committee,

EDWARD COOK, *Chairman.*

To the Commiffioners on ⎰
‘the part of the Union. ⎱

To which the following anfwer was returned.

(No. 5.)

Pittfburg, Auguft 23d, 1794.

GENTLEMEN,

HAVING received affurances of your approbation of the propofitions made by us, and of your determination to recommend them to the people, we have nothing further to add, except to reply to that part of your letter which relates to the Gentlemen from Ohio county.

The whole tenor of our letter of the 21ft inftant, fhews that we had come among you in confequence of the difturbances which had prevailed in the weftern parts of Pennfylvania, to prevent the actual employment of military coercion there, as contemplated in the Prefident's proclamation, and that the late offences referred to, were the infurrections which had prevailed in fome of thefe weftern counties.—We therefore cannot extend our propofitions.

In addition to this, we are well affured, that the people of Ohio county have, not generally authorifed thefe Gentlemen to reprefent them, and we cannot at prefent undertake to make any definite arrangement with them.

We are however, willing to converfe with thefe Gentlemen on this fubject, and we have no doubt, that on fatisfactory proofs of their determination to fupport the laws of their country, and of an intire fubmiffion to them by thofe from whom they come being given, the Prefident will, upon our recommendation, extend a fimilar pardon to any late offences committed againft the United States, if fuch there be committed. We are willing, on receiving such assurances from them, to recommend such application accordingly.

JAMES ROSS,
J. YEATES,
Wm. BRADFORD.

To the Committee }
of Conference. }

The following communication was made to the Commissioners, by the persons said to have been sent from Ohio county, in Virginia.
(No. 6.)

Pittsburg, August 23, 1794.

Gentlemen,

We have seen by your letter of this day, that you have been well assured, that the people of Ohio county did not generally authorise us to represent them. All we have to say on that subject is, that we were authorised fuly* and generally by such persons as met on that accasion. Wheather any of the inhabitance were dissatisfied with our being appointed for that purpose, or wheather there were any who did not wish an appointment to take place at all, we know not ; but we pretent to have no other desine than that of represeting such of the citizens of Ohio county as sent us here.

Waving hower the mear personal subject, we think it a duty we owe our fellow-citizens, to wish (and we know it to have been the opinion of the whole Committee of conference) that no distinction should be made between offences committed upon the same accasion, arising from the same source, and perpetrated at the same time, wheather they happenid in Pennsylvanah or in Virginia ; and we therefore hope you will conceive, it upon full examenation, to be part of your present pacific mission, to satisfy the minds of the people of Virginia as well as thouse of Pennsylvana ; and that you will give assurances that the same proofs which you

---

* The spelling in the foregoing is agreeably to the original.

require from the people of Pennfylvana, of there determination
to fubmit to the laws, fhall be deemed fufficient, when given by
the people of Ohio county to enduce you to recommend to the Prefident to extend a fimilar pardon to any offences committed there
againft the United States ; and that whatever objects you may
have to confider us in the fame point of view with the other members of the Committee of conference, you will not require different conditions from, or propofe different terms to the citizens of
the too ftates, &c.

   We have the honor to be with refpect,
     Gentlemen,
       Your moft obedient and very humble farvants,
        ROBT. STEPHENSON,
        WILLIAM SUTHERLAND,
        Wm. M'KINLEY.

To the Commiffioners ⎱
for the United States. ⎰

(No. 7.)

Gentlemen,

 HAVING converfed with you on the fubject of your letter of
this date, we declare to you, that if the fame declarations and
affurances are made by you, which it is required fhould be made
by the citizens to be affembled at Red-Stone, and if fatisfactory
affurances are alfo given to us of a fincere determination of thofe
individuals in Ohio county who fent you hither, to fubmit to
the laws for raifing a revenue on diftilled fpirits and ftills, on or
before the 14th September next—In fuch cafe we will recommend to the Prefident of the United States, your petition, requefting that a pardon may be granted for any indictable offence againft
the United States, committed in Ohio county fince the 15th day
of July laft, and before the prefent day, on the fame terms offered
to the inhabitants of the fourth furvey of Pennfylvania. But as
certain bonds have been lately taken by force from Zaccheus
Biggs, Collector of the faid Revenue in Ohio county, it is to be

clearly underſtood, that ſaid pardon ſhall not extend to prevent any civil remedy, againſt thoſe who have deſtroyed the ſaid bonds, or are parties to them.

Given under our hands, Auguſt 23, 1794.

> JAMES ROSS,
> J. YEATES,
> Wᴍ. BRADFORD.

To Meſſrs. Robert Stephenſon, }
William Sutherland, and Wil- }
liam M'Kinley. }

To which the following reply was made*.

(No. 8.)

Pittſburg, 23d Aug. 1794.

Gᴇɴᴛʟ.

HAVING Conederd your Letter of this Deate ſince the Departur of the ſpeache Comatie delegated from Weſtmorland Waſhington Featt & Alegunie countis in Penſilvenea & Conidering our Selves a Juſtifyable repentation of thoſe inhabtents of Ohio County by Whowe we were.Deligated & a part of that ſpeachell Comitee to whom your propoſals wear mead and Accepted yeſterday & the day poſding, and relying on the faith alrdy pledged by you and Accepted by the Speachell Comatee we delen entering any further on this Buſſens untell we Conſult our Conſtaituents & the Cometee of Safety.

We are Gentl. with Eſteem your moſt Obed.

> Humble Servt.
> ROBERT STEPHENSON,
> WILLIAM SUTHERLAND
> Wᴍ. M'KINLY.

(No. 9.)

Brownſville, Auguſt 29th, 1794.

Gᴇɴᴛʟᴇᴍᴇɴ,

DIFFICULTIES having ariſen with us, we have thought

---

* The ſpelling in this reply is agreeably to the original.

it neceffary to appoint a Committee to confer with you, in order to procure, if poffible, fome farther time, in order that the people may have *leafure* to reflect upon their true fituation.

I am, Gentlemen,

Your moft obedient humble fervant,

EDWARD COOK.

P. S. Inclofed you have a copy of the refolution on that fubject.

The Hon. the Commiffioners }
   of the United States.   }

(No. 10.)

At a meeting of the ftanding Committee of the weftern counties, held at Brownfville, (Redftone Old-Fort) on the 28th and 29th Auguft 1794—

THE report of the Committee appointed to confer with the Commiffioners of government, being taken into confideration, the following refolutions were adopted, to wit:

1. Refolved, That in the opinion of this Committee, it is the intereft of the people of this country to accede to the propofals made by the Commiffioners on the part of the United States.

Refolved, That a copy of the foregoing refolution be tranfmitted to the faid Commiffioners.

EDW. COOK, *Chairman.*

A true Copy.

ALBERT GALLATIN.

F

The following Letter was delivered to Hugh H. Brackenridge, just before his departure to Redstone (Old Fort) directed " To Messrs. Kirkpatrick, Smith, Powers, D. Bradford, Marshall, Edgar, Cook, Gallatin, Lang, Morton, Lucas and Brackenridge, late conferees."

(No. 11.)

Pittsburg, August 27, 1794.

Gentlemen,

SINCE your departure from Pittsburg, we have transmitted information of our proceedings to the Secretary of State : And it being evident from them that the satisfactory proofs of a sincere submission to the laws cannot be obtained before the 1st September, we may undertake to assure you that the movement of the militia will be suspended until further information is received from us.

We also authorize you to assure the friends of order, who may be disposed to exert themselves to restore the authority of the laws, that they may rely upon all the protection the Government can give ; and that every measure necessary to suppress and punish the violence of ill disposed individuals. who may dissent from the general sentiment (if there should be any such) will be promptly taken in the manner the laws direct.

We are Gentlemen,

Your most humble servants,

JAMES ROSS,
J. YEATES,
Wm. BRADFORD.

——

(No. 12.)

Pittsburg, Sept. 1, 1793.

Gentlemen,

The Committee appointed by the Committee of safety at Redstone the 28th August last, to confer with the Commissioners of the United States and state of Pennsylvania, and agreeable to the refolution of faid Committee, do requeft :

1ft.   That the faid Commiffioners give an affurance on the part of the general government, to an indemnity to all perfons as to the arrearage of excife, that have not entered their ftills to this date.

2d.   Will the Commiffioners aforefaid give to the eleventh day of October next, to take the fenfe of the people at large of the four counties weft of Pennfylvania, and that part of Bedford weft of the Allegheny mountains, and the Ohio county in Virginia, whether they will accede to the refolution of the faid Commiffioners as ftated at large in the conference with the Committee of conference met at Pittfburgh, the 21ft day of Auguft laft.

By order of the Committee,

JOHN M'CLELLAND.

The honorable the Commiffioners ⎫
   on the part of the United States ⎬
   and of the ftate of Pennfylvania. ⎭

(No. 13.)

Pittfburg, September 1ft, 1794.

GENTLEMEN,

WE have received your letter of this date ; and as time preffes have determined to give it an immediate anfwer, although we fhall be prevented thereby, from making fo full and correct a reply, as the importance of the fubject requires.

In our correfpondence with the late Committee of conference, we detailed thofe affurances of fubmiffion to the laws, which would have been deemed full and fatisfactory, and which were neceffary to the exercife of the powers vefted in us.   This detail was minutely fettled in a conference with a fub-committee of that body.   From a defire on our part to accommodate and to render the propofals as unexceptionable as poffible, they were altered and modified at their requeft, 'till being fuperior to all exception, they received the unanimous approbation of thofe gentlemen,

The detail thus fettled required from the ftanding Committee affurances of their explicit determination to fubmit to the laws of the United States ;—that they would not directly or indirectly oppose the execution of the acts for raising a revenue upon distilled spirits and upon stills ; and that they would support, as far as the laws require, the civil authority, in affording the protection due to all officers and other citizens. These assurances have not been given. On the contrary, we learn, with emotions difficult to be repressed, that in the meeting of the Committee at Redstone resistance to the laws and open rebellion against the United States, were publicly advocated, and that two fifths of that body, representing twenty-three townships, totally disapprove the proposals, and preferred the convulsions of a civil contest to the indulgence offered them by their country. Even the members composing the majority, although, by a *secret* and *undistinguishing* vote, they expressed an opinion, that it was the *interest* of the people to accede to the proposals, did not themselves accede to them, nor give the assurances, nor make the recommendations explicitly required of them. They have adjourned without day, and the terms are broken on their part.

We had reason for requiring these declarations and recommendations from that body. They were a representation (in *fact*,) of the different townships of the western counties—they were a body in whom the people had chosen to place confidence—there were among them men, whose advice and example have had influence in misleading the people, and it was proper they should be instrumental in recalling them to their duty : and an avowed determination to support the civil authority in protecting the officers, would have assisted in repressing the violence of turbulent individuals.

Our expectations have been unfortunately disappointed : The terms required have not been acceded to. You have been sent hither to demand new terms ;—and it is now necessary for us to decide, whether we will return home, or enter into other arrangements.

Upon reflection, we are satisfied, that the President of the United States, while he demands satisfactory proofs that there will be in future a perfect submission to the laws, does not wish the great body of the people fhould be finally concluded by the conduct or proceedings of that Committee : and if the people *themfelves* will make the declarations required of the ftanding committee, and give fatisfactory proofs of a general and fincere determination to obey the laws, the benefits offered may ftill be obtained by thofe individuals, who fhall explicitly avow their fubmiffion as herein after mentioned.

It is difficult to decide in what manner the faid declarations and determinations of the people to fubmit peaceably fhould be taken and afcertained. We have thought much on this fubject, and are fully fatisfied, that a decifion by ballot will be wholly unfatisfactory, and that it will be eafy to produce by that means, an apparent but delufive unanimity. It is therefore neceffary, that the determination of every individual be publicly announced. In a crifis, and on a queftion like this, it is difhonorable to temporize. Every man ought to declare himfelf openly, and give his affurances of fubmiffion in a manner that cannot be queftioned hereafter. If a civil conteft muft finally take place, the government ought to know not only the numbers, but the names of the faithful citizens, who may otherwife be in danger of being confounded with the guilty.—It therefore remains with you to fay, whether you will *recommend* fuch a mode of proceedure and will immediately arrange with us the manner in which the fenfe of the people may be publicly taken and written affurances of fubmiffion obtained, within the time already limited. We defire an explicit and fpeedy anfwer in writing.

You requeft us " to give affurances on the part of the United States, that an indemnity fhall be granted as to the arrears of excife, to all perfons that have not entered their ftills to this date." If it were proper to remit all arrears of duty, we cannot conceive why thofe who have entered their ftills, fhould not receive a fimilar indulgence with thofe who have refufed to do fo ; nor why you demand peculiar favors for the oppofers of the acts, while you abandon thofe who have complied, to the ftrictnefs of the laws.

We have gone on that fubject as far as we think advifeable.

The claufe was introduced at the requeft of the late Committee of conference ; and even the ftile of expreffing it was fettled with them. We therefore have nothing more to add to that fubject.

You require alfo that time be given until the 11th day of October, in order to afcertain the fenfe of the people.—That is wholly inadmiffible. On the day of the conference, the time allowed was deemed fufficiently long ; and we are forry to perceive, that delay only tends to produce an indifpofition to decide. There are ftrong reafons, obvious to a reflecting mind, againft prolong-ing the time a fingle hour. Nothing is required but a declaration of that duty which every man owes to his country, and every man before this day muft have made up his mind on the fubject. Six weeks have already elapfed fince the ordinary exercife of civil au-thority has been forcibly fuppreffed, the officers of government expelled, and the perfons and property of well difpofed citizens expofed to the outrages of popular violence. The protection which is due to peaceable citizens—the refpect which every go-vernment owes itfelf—and the great interefts of the United States demand that the authority of the laws be quickly reftored. To this we may add, that the militia, (which by late orders from the Prefident have been increafed to 15,000 men including 1500 rifle-men from Virginia, under the command of Maj. Gen. Morgan) have received orders to affemble, and we cannot undertake to promife that their march will be long fufpended. All poffible means to inform, to conciliate, and to recall our fellow citizens to their duty, have been ufed. If their infatuation ftill continues, we regret, but are perfuaded that further moderation and forbear-ance will increafe it.

If the whole country fhall declare its determination peaceably to fubmit, the hopes of the Executive will be fulfilled : but if a part of the inhabitants of the furvey fhall perfift in their unjuftifi-able refiftance to the lawful authority of the United States, it is not the intention of the government to confound the innocent with the guilty ;—you may therefore affure the friends of order and the laws, that they may rely upon promptly receiving all the protection the government can give ; and that effectual meafures will be taken to fupprefs and punifh the violence of thofe individuals who may endeavour to obftruct the execution of the laws, and to involve their country in a fcene of calamity, the extent and ferioufnefs of which it is impcffible to calculate.

It is eafy to perceive from the whole fcope of this letter, that no part of it is addreffed to. the gentlemen of Ohio county, in Virginia.

JAMES ROSS,
J. YEATES,
Wᴍ. BRADFORD.

To Robert Dickey, John Probft, John Nefbitt, John Marfhel, David Philips, John M'Cleland, George Wallace, and Samuel Wilfon.

(No. 14.)

Pittfburg, September 2, 1794.

Gᴇɴᴛʟᴇᴍᴇɴ,

WE have received your letter of yefterday, and after having duly confidered its contents, we are all of opinion that it is the intereft and duty of the people in the weftern counties of Pennfylvania, to fubmit to the execution of the laws of the United States, and of the ftate of Pennfylvania, upon the principles and terms ftated by the Commiffioners ; and we will heartily recommend this meafure to them. We are alfo ready to enter into the detail with you of fixing and afceitaining the time, place, and manner of collecting the fenfe of the people upon this very momentous fubject.

Signed by the unanimous order of the Committee,

JOHN M'CLELAND.

To the Commiffioners of the United States, and of the ftate of Pennfylvania.

(No. 15.)

At a conference between the Commissioners from the United States and the State of Pennsylvania, on the one part, and Messrs. Probst, Dickey, Nesbit, Marshel, Philips, M'Cleland, Wallace and Wilson, conferees appointed by the standing Committee, at Brownsville, (Redstone Old-Fort) on the 28th and 29th day of August 1794, it was agreed, that the assurances required from the citizens in the fourth survey of Pennsylvania, should be given in writing, and their sense ascertained in the following manner.—

1. THAT the citizens of the said survey, (Allegheny county excepted) of the age of eighteen years and upwards, be required to assemble on Thursday the 11th instant, in their respective townships, at the usual place for holding township meetings; and that between the hours of twelve and seven in the afternoon of the same day, any two or more members of the meeting who assembled at Parkinson's ferry on the 14th ultimo, resident in the township, or a justice of the peace of said township, do openly propose to the people assembled the following questions:—" Do you now engage to submit to the laws of the United States, and that you will not hereafter, directly or indirectly, oppose the execution of the acts for raising a revenue upon distilled spirits and stills? And you do also undertake to support, as far as the laws require, the civil authority, in affording the protection due to all officers and other citizens?"—Yea or Nay.

That the said citizens resident in Allegheny county, shall meet in their respective election districts on the said day, and proceed in the same manner as if they were assembled in townships.

That a minute of the number of the yeas and nays be made immediately after ascertaining the same.

That a written or printed declaration of such engagement be signed by all those who vote in the affirmative, of the following tenor, to wit.

" I do *folemnly promife *henceforth to fubmit to the laws of
the United States; that I will not directly nor indirectly oppofe
the execution of the acts for raifing a revenue on diftilled fpirits
and ftills, and that I will fupport, as far as the law requires, the
civil authority in affording the protection due to all officers and
other citizens."

This fhall be figned in the prefence of the faid members or juftices, attefted by him or them, and lodged in his or their hands.

That the faid perfons fo propofing the queftion ftated as aforefaid, do affemble at the refpective county court-houfes on the
13th inftant, and do afcertain and make report of the number of
thofe who voted in the affirmative, in the refpective townfhips or
diftricts, and of the number of thofe who voted in the negative;
together with their opinion, whether there be fuch a general fubmiffion of the people in their refpective counties, that an office of
infpection may be immediately and fafely eftablifhed therein.

That the faid report, opinion and written or printed declarations be tranfmitted to the Commiffioners, or any one of them,
at Union Town, on or before the 16th inftant.

If the faid affurances fhall be bona fide given in the manner prefcribed, the Commiffioners on the part of the United States do
promife and engage in manner following, to wit.——

1. No profecution for any treafon or other indictable offence
againft the United States, committed within the fourth furvey of
Pennfylvania, before the 22d day of Auguft laft, fhall be commenced or profecuted before the 10th day of July next, againft
any perfon who fhall within the time limited fubfcribe fuch affurance and engagement as aforefaid, and perform the fame.

2. On the faid 10th day of July next there fhall be granted a
general pardon and oblivion of all the faid offences, excluding

G

---

* Objections having been made to the words " folemnly" and " henceforth," the Commiffioners by a publication in the Pittfburgh Gazette,
declared their confent to their being ftruck out.

therefrom, neverthelefs, every perfon who fhall refufe or neglect to fubfcribe fuch affurance and engagement in manner aforefaid, or fhall after fuch fubfcription violate the fame, or wilfully obftruct, or attempt to obftruct, the execution of the faid acts, or be aiding or abetting therein.

3. Congrefs having by an act paffed on the 5th day of June laft, authorifed the ftate courts to take cognizance of offences againft the faid acts for raifing a revenue upon diftilled fpirits and ftills, the Prefident has determined that he will direct fuits againft fuch delinquents to be profecuted therein, if upon experiment it be found that local prejudices or other caufes do not obftruct the faithful adminiftration of juftice; but it is to be underftood, that of this he muft be the judge, and that he does not mean by this determination to impair any power vefted in the Executive of the United States.

4. Certain beneficial arrangements for adjufting delinquencies and profecutions for penalties now depending, fhall be made and communicated by the officers appointed to carry the faid acts into execution.

JAMES ROSS,

J. YEATES,

Wm. BRADFORD.

Signed in behalf of the Committee reprefenting the fourth furvey of Pennfylvania, unanimoufly by the members prefent.

JOHN PROBST, ROBERT DICKEY, JOHN NESBITT, DAVID PHILIPS, JOHN MARSHEL, SAMUEL WILSON, GEO WALLACE, JOHN M'CLELLAND.

Pittfburg, September 2, 1794.

WE, the underwritten, do alfo promife, in behalf of the ftate of Pennfylvania, that in cafe the affurances now propofed, fhall be bona fide given and performed, until the 10th day of July next, an act of free and general pardon and oblivion of all treafons, infurrections, arfons, riots, and other offences inferior to riots, committed, counfelled or fuffered, by any perfon or perfons within the four weftern counties of Pennfylvania, fince the 14th day of July laft paft, fo far as the fame concerns the faid ftate, or the government thereof, fhall be then granted ; excluding therefrom every perfon who fhall refufe or neglect to fubfcribe fuch affurance, or who fhall after fuch fubfcription wilfully violate or obftruct the laws of the ftate or of the United States.

THOMAS M'KEAN,
WILLIAM IRVINE.

(No. 16.)

WE, the fubfcribers, members of the Committee who met at Parkefon's Ferry on the 14th Auguft laft, and Juftices of the Peace of the different townfhips in Wafhington county, met this 13th day of September, 1794, do find ourfelves under great embarraffment to exprefs our fentiments and opinions whether there be fuch a general fubmiffion of the people as that an office of infpection may be immediately and fafely eftablifhed in this county: yet we are free to declare, that no oppofition fhall arife from us the underfigned to the excife law, or to any officer appointed under it, and we believe and are of opinion, that a large majority of the inhabitants of the refpective townfhips in this county will acquiefce and fubmit to the faid laws, under a hope and firm belief that the Congrefs of the United States will repeal faid law.

Given under our hands at Wafhington Court-houfe, the 13th of September, 1794.

DAVID BRADFORD, and 27 others.

(No. 17.)

Unity Townfhip, Weftmoreland County, Sept. 15th, 1794.
Sir,

WE prefume you had information of the oppofition we met with by a turbulent banditti at our townfhip-meeting, on the 11th inftant—that they fnatched away the paper from one of the Committee who met at Parkefon's Ferry, when taking in the fubfcription.

On the Saturday following, a number of the inhabitants voluntarily met and fubfcribed the paper propofed by the Commiffioners on the part of government, but the time being fo fhort, the people generally could not have an opportunity of declaring their approbation; but we are of opinion that a great majority of the moft refpectable inhabitants would chearfully agree to fign, had they an opportunity; there are alfo a number of thofe who were active in the oppofition, who came fince forward and figned.

The whole amount of fubfcribers are one hundred and feven. We have fecured fafely the original papers; and fhould it be thought neceffary to have a lift of the names tranfmitted to you, a line addreffed to the Committee of Unity Townfhip, will be duly attended to.

We are with due refpect,
Your moft obedient humble fervants,
GEO. SMITH,
JAMES MONTGOMERY.

JAMES ROSS, Efquire.

(No. 18.)

Union Town, Sept. 16, 1794.

We the fubfcribers having according to refolutions of the Committee of townfhips, for the county of Fayette, acted as judges, on the eleventh inftant, at the meetings of the people of the faid county refpectively convened at the places in the firft, fecond, and third election diftricts, where the general elections are ufually held (no judge or member of the Committee attending from the fourth and laft diftrict, which confifts of the townfhips of Tyrone and Bullfkin) do hereby certify, that five hundred and fixty of the people thus convened on the day aforefaid, did then and there declare their determination to fubmit to the laws of the United States in the manner expreffed by the Commiffioners on the part of the Union, in their letter dated the 22d day of Auguft laft; the total number of thofe who attended on that occafion, being only feven hundred and twenty-one, that is to fay, fomething lefs than one third of the number of citizens of the faid three diftricts. And we do further certify, that from our prevvious knowledge of the difpofition of the general body of the people, and from the anxiety fince difcovered by many, (who, either from not having had notice, or from not having underftood the importance of the queftion, did not attend) to give fimilar affurances of fub-miffion, we are of opinion that the majority of thofe citizens who did not attend are difpofed to behave peaceably and with due fub-miffion to the laws.

> ALBERT GALLATIN,
> WILLIAM ROBERTS,
> GEORGE DIEUTH,
> JAMES WHITE,
> JOHN JACKSON,
> ANDw. RABB,
> THOMAS PATTERSON.

———

DEPARTMENT OF STATE, October 7th, 1794.

I hereby certify, that the aforegoing Report, and the Documents, No. 1—18, inclufive, therein referred to, are truly copied from files in the Office of the Department of State.

> GEO: TAYLOR, jr. Chief Clerk.

—ERRATA.—

The following is the report which was marked No. 17, and ought to have been inserted in the place of the paper which, thro' mistake, is printed in page 51.

WE the subscribers, judges of a general election held in the several townships of the county, for the purpose of ascertaining certain assurances required of the citizens by the Commissioners on the part of the government, and agreed to on the part of the delegates, having met this day, and taken into consideration the returns from said township (true copies of which have been returned to one of the Commissioners) and finding that some gave only general assurances of their submission and disposition for peace, without individually signing the same, and others in number, according to the returns by them respectively made,—DO CERTIFY, that in our opinion, as ill-disposed lawless persons could suddenly assemble and offer violence, it would not be safe in immediately establishing an office of inspection therein.

Given under our hands at the court-house in Greensburgh, this thirteenth day of September, in the year of our Lord one thousand seven hundred and ninety-four.

JAMES McLEAN,
EBENEZAR BRADY,
CLEMENTS BURLEIGH,
HUGH MARTIN,
JOHN DENNISTON,
CHR. FINLEY,
JOHN KIRKPATRICK,
JOHN YOUNG,
JAMES CALDWELL,
JAS. IRWIN,
JAMES BRADY,
JOHN ANDERSON,
JOHN FINDLEY,
JEREMIAH MURAY,
GEORGE AMENT.

BY THE PRESIDENT OF THE UNITED STATES

OF AMERICA

A PROCLAMATION.

WHEREAS from a hope, that the combinations againſt the Conſtitution and Laws of the United States in certain of the weſtern counties of Pennſylvania would yield to time and reflection, I thought it ſufficient, in the firſt inſtance rather to *take meaſures* for calling forth the militia, than immediately to *embody* them ;—but the moment is now come, when the overtures of forgiveneſs with no other condition, than a ſubmiſſion to law, have been only partially accepted—when every form of conciliation, not inconſiſtent with the being of Government, has been adopted without effect ;—when the well diſpoſed, in thoſe counties, are unable by their influence, and example to reclaim the wicked from their fury, and are compelled to aſſociate in their own defence ;—when the proffered lenity has been perverſely miſinterpreted into an apprehenſion, that the citizens will march with reluctance ;—when the opportunity of examining the ſerious conſequences of a treaſonable oppoſition has been employed in propagating principles of anarchy, endeavoring through emiſſaries to alienate the friends of order from its ſupport, and inviting its enemics to perpetrate ſimilar acts of inſurrection ;—when it is manifeſt, that violence would continue to be exerciſed upon every attempt to enforce the laws ;—when therefore Government is ſet at defiance, the conteſt being whether a ſmall portion of the United States ſhall dictate to the whole Union, and at the expenſe of thoſe, who deſire peace, indulge a deſperate ambition. Now therefore I GEORGE WASHINGTON Preſident of the United States, in obedience to that high and irreſiſtible duty conſigned to me by the Conſtitution "to take care that the laws be faithfully executed ;"—deploring that the American name ſhould be, fullied by the outrages of citizens on their own Government ;—commiferating fuch, as remain obftinate from delufion ;—but refolved in perfect reliance on that gracious Providence which fo fignally difplays its goodnefs towards the Country, to reduce the refractory to a due fubordination to the law ;—do hereby declare and make known, that with a fatisfaction, which can be equalled only by the merits of the militia, fummoned into fervice from the States of New Jerfey, Pennfylvania, Maryland, and Virginia, I have received intelligence of their patriotic alacrity, in obeying the call of the prefent, though painful, yet commanding neceffity ; that a force, which according to every reafonable expectation is adequate to the exigency, is already in motion to the fcene of difaffection ;—that thofe who have confided, or fhall confide in the protection of Government, fhall meet full fuccour under the ftandard, and from the arms of the United States ;—that thofe who having offended againft the law have fince intitled themfelves to indemnity will be treated with the moft liberal good faith, if they fhall not have forfeited their claim by any fubfequent conduct ; and that inftructions are given accordingly. And I do moreover exhort all individuals, officers, and bodies of men, to contemplate with abhorrence the meafures, leading directly or indirectly to thofe crimes, which produce this refort to military coercion ;—to check, in their refpective fpheres the efforts of mifguided or defigning men to fubftitute their mifreprefentations in the place of truth and their difcontents in the place of ftable Government ;—and to call to mind, that as the people of the United States have been permitted under the divine favor, in perfect freedom, after folemn deliberation, and in an enlightened age, to elect their own Government ; fo will their gratitude for this ineftimable bleffing be beft diftinguifhed by firm exertions to maintain the Conftitution and the Laws. And laftly I again warn all perfons whomfoever and wherefoever, not to abet, aid or comfort the Infurgents aforefaid, as they will anfwer the contrary at their peril ; and I do alfo require all officers and other citizens according to their feveral duties, as far as may be in their power, to bring under the cognizance of the law all offenders in the premifes.

IN WITNESS whereof I have caufed the feal of the United States of America to be affixed to thefe prefents, and figned the fame with my hand. Done at the City of Philadelphia the twenty fifth day of September one thoufand feven hundred and ninety four, and of the Independence of the United States of America the nineteeneh.

G°. WASHINGTON

By the Prefident,

EDM: RANDOLPH.

True Copy,

GEO. TAYLOR, Jr.

H

*Communication from Gov. Mifflin to the Prefident of the United
States, on the infurrection in the Weftern counties of Pennfylvania.*

SIR,

THE important fubject, which led to our conference on Saturday laft, and the interefting difcuffion that then took place, having fince engaged my whole attention, I am prepared, in compliance with your requeft, to ftate with candor the meafures which, in
my opinion, ought to be purfued by the Commonwealth of Pennfylvania. The circumftances of the cafe evidently require a firm
and energetic conduct on our part, as well as on the part of the
General Government ; but as they do not preclude the exercife
of a prudent and humane policy, I enjoy a fincere gratification in
recollecting the fentiment of regret, with which you contemplated the poffible neceffity of an appeal to arms : For I confefs,
that in manifefting a zealous difpofition to fecure obedience to
the Conftitutions and Laws of our Country, I too fhall ever pre-
fer the inftruments of conciliation to thofe of coercion ; and never,
but in the laft refort, countenance a dereliction of Judiciary authority, for the exertion of military force.

Under the influence of this general fentiment, I fhall proceed,
Sir, to deliver my opinion relatively to the recent riots in the
county of Allegheny, recapitulating, in the firft place, the actual
ftate of the information which I have received. It appears, then,
that the Marfhal of the Diftrict having, without moleftation,
ferved certain procefs, that iffued from a Federal Court, on various citizens who refide in the county of Fayette, thought it proper to profecute a fimilar duty in the county of Allegheny,
with the affiftance, and in the company of Gen. Nevill; the infpector of the Excife for the Weftern Diftrict of Pennfylvania :
that while thus accompanied he fuffered fome infults, and encountered fome oppofition : that confiderable bodies af armed men
having at feveral times, demanded the furrender of Gen. Nevill's
commiffion and papers, attacked and, ultimately, deftroyed his
houfe : that thefe rioters (of whom a few were killed, and many

wounded) having taken the Marſhal and others priſoners, releaſed that officer, in conſideration of a promiſe, that he would ſerve no more proceſs on the weſtern ſide of the Allegheny Mountain: that, under the apprehenſion of violence, Gen. Nevill, before his houſe was deſtroyed, applied to the Judges of Allegheny county for the protection of his property, but the Judges on the 17th day of July, the day on which his houſe was deſtroyed, declared that they could not, in the preſent circumſtances, afford the protection that was requeſted, though they offered to inſtitute proſecutions againſt the offenders; and that Gen. Nevill and the Marſhal, menaced with further outrage by the rioters, had been under the neceſſity of withdrawing from the country. To this outline of the actual information reſpecting the riots, the ſtoppage of the mail may be added, as matter of aggravation; and the propoſed convention of the inhabitants of the neighbouring counties of Pennſylvania and Virginia, as matter of alarm.

Whatever conſtruction may be given, on the part of the United States, to the facts that have been recited, I cannot heſitate to declare on the part of Pennſylvania, that the incompetency of the Judiciary Department of her Government, to vindicate the violated laws, has not at this period been made ſufficiently apparent, and that the military power of the Government ought not to be employed, until its Judiciary authority, after a fair experiment, has proved incompetent to enforce obedience, or to puniſh infractions of the law.

The law having eſtabliſhed a tribunal and preſcribed the mode for inveſtigating every charge, has likewiſe attached to every offence its proper puniſhment. If an opponent of the Exciſe-ſyſtem refuſes or omits to perform the duty which that ſyſtem preſcribes to him, in common with his fellow citizens, his refuſal, or omiſſion, expoſes him to the penalty of the law; but the payment of the penalty expiates the legal offence. If a riot is committed in the courſe of a reſiſtance to the execution of any law, the rioters expoſe themſelves to the proſecution and puniſhment, but the fufferance of their fentence extinguifhes their crime. In either inftance, however, if the ftrength and audacity of a lawlefs combination fhall baffle and deftroy the efforts of the Judiciary authority to recover a penalty, or to inflict a punifhment, that authority may conftitutionally claim the auxiliary intervention of a military power; but ftill the intervention cannot commence 'till the impotency of the Judicial authority has been proved by experiment, nor continue a moment longer than the occafion for which it was exprefsly required. That the laws of the Union are the laws of the ftate, is a Conftitutional axiom that will never be controverted : that the authority of the ftate ought to be exerted in maintaining the authority of the Union, is a patriotic pofition which I have uniformly inculcated :—but in executing the laws or maintaining the authority of the Union, the government of Pennfylvania can only employ the fame means, by which the more peculiarly Municipal laws and authority of the State are executed and maintained. 'Till the Riot was committed, no offence had occurred, which required the aid of the ftate government :— When it was committed, it became the duty of the ftate government to profecute the offenders, as for a breach of the public peace and the laws of the Commonwealth, and if the meafures fhall be precifely what woud have been purfued, had the Riot been unconnected with the fyftem of Federal policy, all I prefume, will be done, which good faith and juftice can require. Had the Riot been unconnected with the fyftem of Federal policy, the vindication of our laws would be left to the ordinary courfe of juftice; and only in the laft refort, at the requifition, and as an auxiliary of the civil authority, would the military force of the ftate be called forth.

Experience furnifhes the ftrongeft inducements to my mind, for perfevering in this lenient courfe. Riots have heretofore been committed in oppofition to the laws of Pennfylvania, but the Rioters have invariably been punifhed by our courts of juftice. In oppofition to the laws of the United States, in oppofition to

the very laws now oppofed, and in the very counties fuppofed to
be combined in the prefent oppofition, riots have, likewife, formerly occurred ; but in every inftance, fupported by legal proof,
the offenders have been indicted, convicted, and punifhed, before
the tribunals of the ftate. This refult does not announce a defect
of jurisdiction—a want of Judicial power, or difpofition to punifh
infractions of the law ; a neceffity for an appeal from the political
to the phyfical ftrength of the nation.

But another principle of policy deferves fome confideration._ In
a free country it muft be expedient to convince the citizens of the
neceffity, that fhall, at any time, induce the government to employ the coercive authority with which it is invefted. To convince them that it is neceffary to call forth the Military power,
for the purpofe of executing the laws, it muft be fhewn, that the
Judicial power has, in vain, attempted to punifh thofe who violate
them : and, therefore, thinking, as I do, that the incompetency
of the Judicial power of Pennfylvania has not yet been fufficiently afcertained, I remarked, in the courfe of our late conference,
that I did not think it would be an eafy tafk to embody the militia
on the prefent occafion. The citizens of Pennfylvania (however
a part of them may, for a while be deluded) are the friends of
law and order : but when the inhabitants of one diftrict fhall be
required to take arms againft the inhabitants of another, their general character does not authorize me to promife a paffive obedience to the mandates of government. I believe, that as freemen
they would enquire into the caufe and nature of the fervice propofed to them ; and, I believe, that their alacrity in performing,
as well as in accepting it, would effentially depend on their opinion of its juftice and neceffity.

Upon great political emergencies, the effect of every meafure
fhould be deliberately weighed. If it fhall be doubted, whether
faying that the Judiciary power is yet untried, is enough to deter
us from the immediate ufe of military force, an anticipation of
the probable confequences of that awful appeal, will enable us

perhaps fatisfactorily to remove or overlook the doubt. Will not
the refort to force enflame and cement the exifting oppofition ?
Will it not affociate, in a common refiftance, thofe who have hitherto peaceably, as well as thofe who have riotoufly, expreffed
their abhorrence of the Excife ? Will it not collect and combine
every latent principle of difcontent, arifing from the fuppofed oppreffive operations of the Federal judiciary, the obftruction of
the Weftern navigation, and a variety of other local fources ?
May not the magnitude of the oppofition, on the part of the ill-
difpofed, or the difsatisfaction at a premature refort to arms, on
the part of the well difpofed citizens of this ftate, eventually involve the neceffity of employing the militia of other ftates ? And
the accumulation of difcontent, which the jealoufy engendered
by that movement may produce, who can calculate, or who will
be able to avert ? Nor, in this view of the fubject, ought we to
omit paying fome regard to the ground for fufpecting, that the
Britifh Government has already, infidioufly and unjuftly, attempted to feduce the citizens on our Weftern frontier from their duty;
and, we know. that in a moment of defperation or difguft, men
may be led to accept that as an afylum, which, under different
impreffions, they would fhun as a fnare. · It will not, I am perfuaded, fir, be prefumed, from the expreffion of thefe fentiments,
that I am infenfible to the indignation, which the late outrages
ought to excite in the mind of a Magiftrate, entrufted with the
execution of the laws. My object, at prefent, is to demonftrate,
that on the principles of policy, as well as of law, it would be
improper in me to employ the military power of the ftate, while
its judiciary authority is competent to punifh the offenders. But
fhould the judiciary authority prove infufficient, be affured of the
moft vigorous co-operation of the whole force which the Conftitution and Laws of the State entruft to me, for the purpofe of
compelling a due obedience to the Government ; and, in that unfortunate event, convinced that every other expedient has been
reforted to in vain, the public opinion will fanctify our meafures,

and every honeſt citizen will willingly lend his aid to ſtrengthen and promote them.

The ſteps which under my inſtructions were taken, as ſoon as the intelligence reſpecting the riots was received, will clearly, indeed, manifeſt the ſenſe that I entertain upon the ſubject. To every Judge, Juſtice, Sheriff, Brigade Inſpector, in ſhort to every public officer reſiding in the Weſtern counties, a letter was addreſſed expreſſing my indignation and regret, and requiring an exertion of their influence and authority to ſuppreſs the tumults and puniſh the offenders.

The Attorney General of the ſtate was, likewiſe, deſired to inveſtigate the circumſtances of the riot, to aſcertain the names of the rioters, and to inſtitute the regular proceſs of the law, for bringing the leaders to juſtice. In addition to theſe preliminary meaſures, I propoſe iſſuing a Proclamation, in order to declare (as far as I can declare them) the ſentiments of the Government; to announce a determination to proſecute and puniſh the offenders; and to exhort the citizens at large to purſue a peaceable and patriotic conduct: I propoſe engaging three reſpectable citizens to act as Commiſſioners for addreſſing thoſe who have embarked in the preſent combination, upon the lawleſs nature, and ruinous tendency of their proceedings; for inculcating the neceſſity of an immediate return to the duty which they owe to their country; and for promiſing (as far as the ſtate is concerned) a forgiveneſs of their paſt tranſgreſſions, upon receiving a ſatisfactory aſſurance that, in future, they will ſubmit to the laws: and I propoſe, if all theſe expedients ſhould be abortive, to convene the Legiſlature, that the ultimate means of ſubduing the ſpirit of inſurrection, and of reſtoring tranquillity and order, may be preſcribed by their wiſdom and authority.

You will perceive, ſir, that throughout my obſervations, I have cautiouſly avoided any reference to the nature of the evidence, from which the facts that relate to the riots are collected, or to the conduct which the Government of the United States may purfue on this important occafion. I have hitherto, indeed, only fpoken as the Executive Magiftrate of Pennfylvania, charged with a general fuperintendance and care that the laws of the Commonwealth be faithfully executed, leaving it as I ought implicitly to your judgment, to chufe on fuch evidence as you approve, the meafures for difcharging the analogous truft which is confided to you in relation to the laws of the Union. But before I conclude, it is proper under the impreffion of my Federal obligations, to add a full and unequivocal affurance, that whatever requifition you may make, whatever duty you may impofe, in purfuance of your conftitutional and legal powers, will on my part be promptly undertaken, and faithfully difcharged.

I have the honor to be,
With perfect refpect,
Sir,
Your Excellency's
Moft obedient humble fervant,

THO. MIFFLIN.

True Copy.

GEORGE TAYLOR, Jr.

Philadelphia,
5th Auguft 1794.

To the Prefident of the United States.

COMMUNICATION *from the Secretary of State to Governor Mifflin, in anfwer to his of 5th Auguft to the Prefident of the United States.*

DEPARTMENT OF STATE,

Auguft 7th, 1794.

SIR,

THE Prefident of the United States has directed me to acknowledge the receipt of your letter of the 5th inftant and to communicate to you the following reply.

In requefting an interview with you on the fubject of the recent difturbances in the weftern parts of Pennfylvania the Prefident, befides the defire of manifefting a refpectful attention to the Chief Magiftrate of a State immediately affected, was influenced by the hope, that a free conference guided by a united and comprehenfive view of the Conftitutions of the United States and of Pennfylvania, and of the refpective inftitutions, authorities, rights, and duties of the two Governments would have affifted him in forming more precife ideas of the nature of the co-operation, which could be eftablifhed between them, and a better judgment of the plan, which it might be advifeable for him to purfue, in the execution of his truft in fo important and delicate a conjuncture. This having been his object, it is matter of fome regret, that the courfe, which has been fuggefted by you, as proper to be purfued, feems to have contemplated Pennfylvania in a light too feparate and unconnected. The propriety of that courfe, in moft, if not in all refpects, would be fufceptible of little queftion if there were no Fœderal Government,

I

Fœderal Laws, Fœderal Judiciary, or Fœderal Officers; if important laws of the United States, by a feries of violent, as well as of artful expedients, had not been fruftrated in their execution for more than three years; if Officers immediately charged with that execution, after fuffering much and repeated infult, abufe, perfonal ill treatment, and the deftruction of property, had not been compelled for fafety to fly the places of their refidence, and the fcenes of their official duties; if the fervice of the proceffes of a Court of the United States, had not been refifted, the Marfhal of the Diftrict made and detained for fome time prifoner, and compelled for fafety alfo to abandon the performance of his duty, and return by a circuitous route to the feat of Government;—if in fine, a Judge of the United States had not in due form of law notified to the Prefident, " that in the counties of Wafhington " and Alleghany, in Pennfylvania, laws of the United States " are oppofed, and the execution thereof obftructed, by com- " binations too powerful to be fuppreffed by the ordinary " courfe of Judicial proceedings or by the powers vefted in " the Marfhal of that Diftrict." It is true, your Excellency has remarked that in the plan fuggefted, you have only fpoken as the Executive Magiftrate of Pennfylvania, charged with a general fuperintendance and care, that the laws of the Commonwealth be fully executed, leaving it implicitly to the judgment of the Prefident to choofe, on fuch evidence as he approves, the meafures for difcharging the analogous truft, which is confided to him in relation to the laws of the Union. But it is impoffible not to think that the current of the obfervations in your letter, efpecially as to the confequences which may refult from the employment of coercive meafures previous to the preliminary courfe which is indicated in it, may be conftrued to imply a virtual difapprobation of that plan of conduct on the part of the General Government in the actual

ftage of its affairs, which you acknowledge would be proper
on the part of the Government of Pennfylvania if arrived at
a fimilar ftage. Let it be affumed here (to be more particularly fhewn hereafter) that the Government of the United
States is now at that point, where it is admitted, if the Government of Pennfylvania was, the employment of force, by
its authority, would be juftifiable—And let the following
extracts be confulted for the truth of the inference which has
been juft expreffed—" Will not the refort to force inflame
" and cement the exifting oppofition ? Will it not affociate
" in a common refiftance thofe who have hitherto peaceably,
" as well as thofe who have riotoufly, expreffed their abhor-
" rence of the Excife ? Will it not collect and combine every
" latent principle of difcontent, arifing from the fuppofed
" oppreffive operations of the Fœderal Judiciary, the ob-
" ftruction of the weftern navigation and a variety of other
" local fources ? May not the magnitude of the oppofition on
" the part of the ill difpofed, or the diffatisfaction of a *prema-*
" *ture refort to arms* on the part of the well difpofed citizens
" of the State, eventually involve the neceffity of employing
" the militia of other States ? And the accumulation of dif-
" content which the jealoufy engendered by that movement
" may produce who can calculate, or who will be able to
" avert ?"

These important queftions naturally give birth to the following ferious reflections. The iffue of human affairs are in
the hand of Providence. Thofe entrufted with them in Society have no other fure guide than the fincere and faithful
difcharge of their duty, according to the beft of their judgment.
In emergencies great and difficult, not to act with an energy
proportioned to their magnitude and preffure, is as dangerous
as any other conceivable courfe. In the prefent cafe, not to

exert the means, which the laws prefcribe for effectuating their own execution, would be to facrifice thofe Laws, and with them the Conftitution, the Government, the principles of focial Order, and the Bulwarks of private right and fecurity. What worfe can happen from the exertion of thofe means ?

If, as cannot be doubted, the great Body of the Citizens of the United States are attached to the Conftitution, which they have eftablifhed for the management of their common concerns—If they are refolved to fupport their own Authority in that of the Conftitutional Laws, againft diforderly and violent combinations of comparatively fmall portions of the Community—If they are determined to protect each other in the enjoyment of fecurity to perfon and property—If they are decided to preferve the Character of Republican Government, by evincing that it has adequate refources for maintaining the Public Order :—If they are perfuaded, that their fafety and their welfare, are materially connected with the prefervation of the Union, and confequently of a Government adequate to its exigencies :—In fine, if they are difpofed to continue that ftate of refpectability and profperity, which is now defervedly the admiration of mankind—the enterprife to be accomplifhed, fhould a refort to force prove inevitable, though difagreeable and painful, cannot be arduous or alarming.

If, in addition to thefe difpofitions in the community at large, the officers of the governments of the refpective States, feeling it to be not only a patriotic, but a Conftitutional duty (inculcated by the oath enjoined upon all the officers of a State, Legiflative, Executive and Judicial) to fupport in their feveral ftations, the Conftitution of the United States— fhall be difpofed as occafion may require (a thing as little to be doubted as the former) with sincerity and good Faith to co-operate with the government of the United States to second with all their influence and weight its legal and necessary measures by a real and substantial concert; then the enterprise to be accomplished can hardly ever be deemed difficult.

But if, contrary to the anticipations which are entertained of these favorable disposition, the great body of the people should be found indifferent to the preservation of the government of the Union, or insensible to the necessity of vigorous exertions to repel the danger, which threatens their most important interests ; or if an unwillingness to encounter partial inconveniences should interfere with the discharge of what they owe to their permanent welfare; or if either yielding to the suggestions of particular prejudices, or misled by the arts which may be employed to infuse jealousy and discontent, they should suffer their zeal for the support of public order to be relaxed by an unfavorable opinion of the merits and tendency of the measures, which may be adopted ; if above all, it were possible that any of the State governments should, instead of prompting the exertions of the citizens, assist directly or indirectly in damping their ardor, by giving a wrong bias to their judgment, or by disseminating dissatisfaction with the proceedings of the general Government, or should counteract the success of those proceedings by any sinister influence whatever,—then indeed, no one can calculate, or may be able to avert, the fatal evils with which such a state of things would be pregnant. Then indeed, the foundations of our political happiness may be deeply shaken, if not altogether overturned.

The President, however, can suppose none of these things. He cherishes an unqualified confidence in the virtue and good fenfe of the people, in the integrity and patriotifm of the officers of the State Governments—and he counts abfolutely on the fame affectionate fupport, which he has experienced upon all former occafions, and which he is confcious that the goodnefs of his intentions now, not lefs than heretofore, merits.

It has been promifed to fhew more particularly hereafter, that the government of the United States is now at that point, where it is confeffed, if the State Government was, the employment of force on its part, would be juftifiable. This promife remains to be fulfilled.

The facts already noted, eftablifh the conclufion, but to render it palpable, it will be of ufe to apply them to the pofitions which your Excellency has been pleafed to lay down.

You admit that, as the offences committed, refpect the State, the military power of the government ought to be employed, where its judiciary authority, after a fair experiment, had proved incompetent to enforce obedience or to punifh infractions of the law, that if the ftrength and audacity, of a lawlefs combination fhall baffle and deftroy the efforts of the judiciciary authority, to recover a penalty or inflict a punifhment, that authority may conftitutionally claim the auxilliary intervention of the military power;—that in the laft refort, at the requifition, and as an auxiliary of the civil authority the military force of the State would be called forth. And you declare, that the circumftances of the cafe evidently require a firm and energetic conduct on the part both of State and general Government.

For more than three years, as already obferved, certain laws of the United States have been obftructed in their execution, by diforderly combinations. Not only officers, whofe immediate duty it was to carry them into effeƐ, have fuffered violent perfonal outrage and injury, and deftruƐion of property, at different times, but fimilar perfecution has been extended to private citizens, who have aided, countenanced, or only complied with the laws. The violences committed have been fo frequent and fuch in their degree as to have been matter of general notoriety and alarm—and it may be added, that they have been abundantly within the knowledge and under the notice of the Judges and Marfhals of Pennfylvania, of fuperior as well as of inferior jurifdiƐion. If in particular inftances, they have been punifhed by the exertions of the magiftrates, it is at leaft certain, that their effeƐs have been in the main ineffeƐual. The fpirit, has continued, and, with fome intervals of relaxation, has been progreffive, manifefting itfelf in reiterated exceffes. The Judiciary authority of the United States has alfo, prior to the attempt, which preceded the late crifis, made fome fruitlefs efforts under a former Marfhal,—an officer fent to execute procefs was deterred from it, by the manifeft danger of proceeding. Thefe particulars ferve to explain, the extent, obftinacy, and inveteracy of the evil.

But the faƐs which immediately decide the complexion of the exifting crifis, are thefe. Numerous delinquencies exifted, with regard to a compliance with the laws laying duties on fpirits diftilled within the United States and upon ftills. An armed banditti, in difguife, had recently gone to the houfe of an Officer of the Revenue in the night, attacked it, broken open the doors, and by menaces of inftant death enforced by piftols prefented at him, had compelled a furrender of his Commiffion, and Books of Office. Cotemporary aƐs of violence had been perpetrated in other quarters. Proceffes iffued out of a Court of the United States to recover the penalties incident to non-compliance with the laws, and to bring to punifhment the violent infractors of them, in the abovementioned cafe, againft two of whom indictments had been found. The Marfhal of the Diftrict went in perfon to execute thefe proceffes. In the courfe of his duty, he was actually fired upon on the high road, by a body of armed men. Shortly after other bodies of armed men (in the laft inftance amounting to feveral hundred perfons) repeatedly attacked the houfe of the Infpector of the Revenue with the declared intention of compelling him to renounce his office, and of obftructing the execution of the laws. One of thefe bodies of armed men made prifoner of the Marfhal of the diftrict, put him in jeopardy of his life, and did not releafe him till for fafety, and to obtain his liberty, he engaged to forbear the further execution of the proceffes with which he was charged. In confequence of further requifitions and menaces of the infurgents, the Marfhal, together with the Infpector of the Revenue, have been fince under the neceffity of flying fecretly, and by a circuitous route, from the fcene of thefe tranfactions, towards the feat of government.

An affociate Juftice, purfuant to the provifions of the Laws for that purpofe, has; in the manner already ftated, officially notified the Prefident of the exiftence of combinations in two of the counties of this State to obftruct the execution of the laws, too powerful to be fuppreffed by the judiciary authority, or by the powers of the Marfhal.

Thus then is it unequivocally, and in due form, afcertained in reference to the Government of the United States, that the Judiciary Authority, after a fair and full experiment, has proved incompetent to enforce obedience to, or to punifh infractions of the Laws—that the ftrength and audacity of certain lawlefs combinations have baffled and deftroyed the efforts of the Judiciary Authority to recover penalties or inflict punifhment, and that this authority, by a regular notification of this ftate of things, has in the laft refort, as an auxiliary of the Civil Authority, claimed the intervention of the military power of the United States. It refults from thefe facts, that the cafe exifts, when according to the pofitions advanced by your Excellency in reference to the State Government, the military power may, with due regard to all the requifite cautions, be rightfully interpofed. And that the interpofition of this power is called for, not only by principles of a firm, and energetic conduct, on the part of the General Government, but by the indifpenfable duty, which the Conftitution and the Laws prefcribe to the Executive of the United States.

In this conclufion, your Excellency's difcernment on mature reflection, cannot, it is prefumed, fail to acquiefce—nor can it refufe its concurrence in the opinion which the Prefident entertains, that he may reafonably expect when called for, the zealous co-operation of the Militia of Pennfylvania—that as Citizens, Friends to Law and Order, they may comply with the call without any thing that can properly be denominated " a paffive obedience to the *mandates* of Government," and that as Freemen, judging rightly of the caufe and nature of the fervice propofed to them, they will feel themfelves under the moft facred of obligations to accept and to perform it with alacrity. The theory of our political inftitutions knows no difference between the obligations of our Citizens in fuch a cafe, whether it relate to the Government of the Union or of a State—and it is hoped and confided, that a difference will be as little known to their affections or opinions.

Your Excellency, it is alfo prefumed, will as little doubt, on the like mature reflexion, that in fuch a cafe the Prefident could not without an abdication of the undoubted rights and authorities of the United States and of his duty, poftpone

K

the meafures, for which the Laws of the United States provide, to a previous experiment of the plan which is deline-
ated in your letter.

The people of the United States have eftablifhed a Government for the management of their general Interefts. They
have inftituted executive Organs for adminiftering that Government; and their Reprefentatives have eftablifhed the
Rules by which thofe Organs are to act. When their authority in that of their Government is attacked, by lawlefs
combinations of the Citizens of part of a ftate, they could
never be expected to approve that the care of vindicating
their Authority, of enforcing their Laws, fhould be transferred from the officers of their own Government to thofe
of a ftate—and this to wait the iffue of a procefs fo undeter-
minate in its duration, as that which it is propofed to purfue;
comprehending a further and full experiment of the judiciary
Authority of the State, a Proclamation " to declare the fentiments of its Government, announce a determination to
profecute and punifh offenders, and to exhort the Citizens at
large to purfue a peaceable and patriotic conduct"—the fending of Commiffioners " to addrefs thofe who have embarked
in the prefent combinations upon the lawlefs nature and ruinous tendency of their proceedings, to inculcate the neceffity
of an immediate return to the duty which they owe their
country, and to promife, as far as the ftate is concerned,
forgivenefs of their paft tranfactions upon receiving a fatisfactory affurance that in future they will fubmit to the laws"—
and finally, a call of the Legiflature of Pennfylvania, " that
the ultimate means of fubduing the fpirit of infurrection and
of reftoring tranquility and order may be prefcribed by their
wifdom and authority."

If there were no other objection to a transfer of this kind,
the very important difference which is fuppofed to exift in

the nature and confequences of the offences that have been committed in the contemplation of the Laws of the United States, and of thofe of Pennfylvania, would alone be a very ferious obftacle.

The paramount confiderations, which forbid an acquiefcence in this courfe of proceeding render it unneceffary to difcufs the probability of its fuccefs ;—elfe it might have been proper to teft the confiderations, which have been mentioned as a ground of hope, by the inquiry what was the precife extent of the fuccefs of paft experiments—and efpecially whether the execution of the Revenue laws of Pennfylvania within the fcene in queftion was truly, and effectually accomplifhed by them, or whether they did not rather terminate in a tacit compromife, by which appearances only were faved.

You are already, Sir, advifed that the Prefident, yielding to the impreffions which have been ftated has determined to take meafures for calling forth the militia and that thefe meafures contemplate the affembling a body of between twelve and thirteen thoufand men from Pennfylvania, and the neighboring ftates of Virginia, Maryland and New-Jerfey. The recourfe thus early to the militia of the neighboring ftates proceeds from a probability of the infufficiency of that of Pennfylvania alone, to accomplifh the object; your Excellency having in your conference with the Prefident confirmed the conclufion, which was deducible from the known local and other circumftances of the ftate, by the frank and exprefs declaration which you made of your conviction of that infufficiency, in reference to the number which could be expected to be drawn forth for the purpofe.

But while the Prefident has conceived himfelf to be under an indifpenfable obligation to prepare for that eventual refort, he has ftill confulted the fentiment of regret which he expreffed to you, at the poffible neceffity of an appeal to arms;

and to avert it, if practicable, as well as to manifest his attention to the principle, that " a firm and energetic conduct
does not preclude the exercise of a prudent and humane
policy"—he has (as you have been also advised) concluded
upon the measure of sending himself Commissioners to the
discontented counties to make one more experiment of a
conciliatory appeal to the reason, virtue and patriotism of
their inhabitants, and has also signified to you how agreeable
would be to him your co-operation in the same expedient, which
you have been pleased to afford.   It can scarcely be requisite
to add, that there is nothing he has more at heart, than that
the issue of this experiment, by establishing the authority of
the laws, may preclude the always calamitous necessity of an
appeal to arms.   It would plant a thorn in the remainder of
his path through life to have been obliged to employ force
against fellow-citizens, for giving solidity and permanency to
blessings, which it has been his greatest happiness, to co-operate with them in procuring for a much loved country.

The President receives with much pleasure the assurance
you have repeated to him, that whatever requisition he may
make, whatever duty he may impose, in pursuance of his
Constitutional and legal powers, will on your part be promptly undertaken and faithfully discharged ; and acknowledging,
as an earnest of this and even more, the measures of co-operation which you are pursuing, he assures you in return, that
he relies fully on the most cordial aid and support from you
in every way, which the Constitutions of the United States
and of Pennsylvania, shall authorise and present or future exigencies may require.

And he requests that you will construe, with a reference
to this assurance of his confidence, whatever remarks may
have been made in the course of this reply to your letter ; if

it fhall have happened that any of them have erred, through a mifconception of the fentiments and views which you may have meant to commnnicate.

    With perfeft refpeft, I have the honor to be
        Sir,
            Your moft obedient fervant,

                    EDM. RANDOLPH.
                    Secretary of State.

        (True Copy)
            GEO. TAYLOR, Jr.

Auguft 7th, 1794.

    His Excellency
        Governor Mifflin. }

COMMUNICATION *from Governor Mifflin, to the President of the United States in answer to the Secretary of State's of 7th August.*

S I R,

The Secretary of State has tranfmitted to me, in a letter dated the 7th of Auguft (but only received yefterday) your reply to my letter of the 5th inftant.

For a variety of reafons, it might be defirable at this time, to avoid an extenfion of our correfpondence upon the fubject to which thofe letters particularly relate ; but the nature of the remarks contained in your reply, and the fincerity of my defire to merit, on the cleareft principles, the confidence, which you are pleafed to repofe in me, will juftify, even under the prefent circumftances of the cafe, an attempt to explain any ambiguity, and to remove any prejudice, that may have arifen, either from an inaccurate expreffion, or an accidental mifconception, of the fentiments and views, which I meant to communicate.

That the courfe, which I have fuggefted as proper to be purfued, in relation to the recent difturbances in the weftern parts of Pennfylvania, contemplates the State, in a light too feparate and unconnected, is a pofition, that I certainly did not intend to fanction, in any degree, that could wound your mind with a fentiment of regret. In fubmitting the conftruction of the facts, which muft regulate the operation of the General Government, implicitly to your judgment ;—in cautioufly avoiding any reference to the nature of the evidence, from which thofe facts are collected, or to the conduct which the Government of the United States might purfue ;—in declaring that I fpoke only as the Executive Magiſtrate of the State, charged with the general fuperintendance and care, that its laws be faithfully executed ;—and, above all, in giving a full and unequivocal aſſurance, that whatever requiſition you may make, whatever duty you may impoſe, in purſuance of your conſtitutional and legal powers, would, on my part, be promptly undertaken, and faithfully diſcharged ; I thought that I had manifeſted the ſtrongeſt fenſe of my federal obligations ; and that, ſo far from regarding the State in a feparate and unconnected light, I had exprefsly recognized the fubjection of her individual authority, to the national juriſdiction of the Union.

It is true, however, Sir, that I have only ſpoken as the Executive Magiſtrate of the State ; but, in that character, it is a high gratification to find, that according to your opinion, likewife, " the propriety of the courſe which I fuggeſted, would in moſt if not in all reſpects, be fufceptible of little queſtion." Permit me then, to aſk, in what other character could I have ſpoken, or what other language did the occafion require to be employed ? If the co-operation of the Government of Pennſylvania was the object of our conference, your conſtitutional requiſition as the Executive of the Union, and my official compliance as the Executive of the State, would indubitably enſure it ; but, if a preliminary, a feparate, an unconnected conduct was expected to be purſued by the Executive Magiſtrate of Pennſylvania, his feparate and unconnected power and diſcretion muſt furniſh the rule of proceeding ; and by that rule, agreeably to the admiſſion which I have cited, " the propriety of my courſe would in moſt, if not in all, reſpects, be fufceptible of little queſtion." It muſt, therefore, in juſtice be remembered, that a principal point in our conference, related to the expediency of my adopting, independent of the General Government, a *preli-*

minary meafure (as it was then termed) under the authority of an Act of the Legiflature of Pennfylvania, which was paffed on the 22d of September 1783 and which the Attorney General of the United States thought to be in force, but which had, in fact, been repealed, on the 11th of April 1793.

Upon the ftricteft idea of co-operative meafures, however, I do not conceive, Sir, that any other plan could have been fuggefted confiftently with the powers of the Executive Magiftrate of Pennfylvania, or with a reafonable attention, on my part, to a fyftematic and energetic courfe of proceeding. The complicated nature of the outrage, which was committed upon the public peace, gave a jurifdiction to both Governments; but in the mode of profecuting, or in the degree of punifhing the offenders, that circumftance could not, I apprehend, alter or enlarge the powers of either. The State (as I obferved in my laft letter) could only exert itfelf in executing the laws or maintaining the authority of the Union, by the fame means which fhe employed to execute and maintain her more peculiarly municipal laws and authority; and hence I inferred, and ftill venture to infer, that if the courfe which I have fuggefted is the fame that would have been purfued, had the riot been unconnected with the fyftem of Federal policy, its propriety cannot be rendered queftionable, merely by taking into our view (what I never have ceafed to contemplate) the exiftence of a Federal Government, Federal Laws, Federal Judiciary and Federal Officers. But would it have been thought more confonant with the principle of co-operation, had I iffued orders for an immediate, a feparate, and an unconnected call of the militia, under the fpecial authority which was fuppofed to be given by a law, or under the general authority which may be prefumed to refult from the Conftitution? Let it be confidered, that you had already determined to exercife your legal powers in drafting a com-

petent force of the militia; and it will be allowed; that if I
had undertaken, not only to comply promptly with your
requisition, but to embody a diftinct corps for the fame fervice, an ufelefs expence would have been incurred by the
State, an unneceffary burthen would have been impofed on
the Citizens; and embarraffment and confufion would probably have been introduced inftead of fyftem and co-operation.
Regarding it in this point of light, indeed it may be natural
to think, that in the Judiciary, as well as the Military
department, the fubject fhould be left entirely to the management, either of the State or of the General Government;
for " the very important difference which is fuppofed to
exift in the nature and confequences of the offences that
have been committed, in the contemplation of the laws of
the United States, and of thofe of Pennfylvania," muft otherwife deftroy that uniformity in the diftinction of crimes, and
the apportionment of punifhments, which has always been
deemed effential to a due adminiftration of juftice.

But let me not, Sir, be again mifunderftood : I no not
mean by thefe obfervations to intimate an opinion or to exprefs a wifh, that " the care of vindicating the authority, or of
enforcing the laws of the Union fhould be transferred from
the officers of the General Govenment, to thofe of the State:"
nor, after exprefsly avowing that I had cautioufly avoided any
reference to the conduct, which the Government of the
United States might purfue on this important occafion, did
I think an opportunity could be found to infer that I was de-
firous of impofing a fufpenfion of your proceedings, for the
purpofe of waiting the iffue of the procefs, which I defigned
to purfue. If indeed, " the Government of the United
States was at that point, where it was admitted, if the Government of Pennfylvania was, the employment of force by
its authority would be juftifiable." I am perfuaded, that, on

L

mature confideration, you will do more credit to my candor, than to fuppofe, that I meant to condemn, or to prevent, the adoption of thofe meafures on the part of the General Government, which in the fame circumftances, I fhould have approved and promoted on the part of Pennfylvania.

The extracts that are introduced into the letter of the Secretary of State, in order to fupport that inference, can only be juftly applied to the cafe which was immediately in contemplation, the cafe of the State of Pennfylvania, whofe judiciary authority had not then, in my opinion, been fufficiently tried: They ought not furely be applied to a cafe which I had cautioufly excluded from my view, the cafe of the United States, whofe judiciary authority had, in your opinion, proved inadequate to the execution of the laws, and the prefervation of order. And if they fhall be thus limited to their proper object, the juftice and force of the argument which flows from them, can never be fuccefsfully controverted or denied. While you, Sir, were treading in the plain path defignated by a pofitive law; with no other care than to preferve the forms which the Legiflature had prefcribed; and relieved from a weight of refponfibility by the legal operation of a Judge's certificate; I was called upon to act, not in conformity to a pofitive law, but in compliance with the duty, which is fuppofed to refult from the nature and conftitution of the Executive Office.

The Legiflature had prefcribed no forms to regulate my courfe;—no certificate to inform my judgment,—every ftep muft be dictated by my own difcretion;—and every error of conftruction or conduct, would be charged on my own character. Hence arofe an effential difference in our official fituations; and, I am confident, that on this ground alone, you will perceive a fufficient motive for my confidering the objection, in point of law to forbear the use of military force, till the judiciary authority has been tried, as well as the probable effects, in point of policy, which that awful appeal might produce.

For, Sir, it is certain, that at the time of our conference, there was no satisfactory evidence of the incompetency of the judicial authority of Pennsylvania, to vindicate the violated laws : I therefore could not, as Executive Magistrate, proceed upon a military plan ; but actuated by the genuine spirit of co-operation, not by a desire to sully the dignity or to alienate the powers of the General Government, I still hoped and expected to be able on this, as on former occasions, to support the Laws of the Union, to punish the violaters of them, by an exertion of the Civil Authority of the State Government, the State Judiciary, and the State Officers. This hope prompted the conciliatory course, which I determined to pursue, and which, so far as respects the appointment of Commissioners, you have been pleased to incorporate with your plan. And if, after all, the purposes of justice could be attained, obedience to the laws could be restored, and the horrors of a civil war could be averted by the auxiliary intervention of the State Government, I am persuaded, you will join me in thinking, that the idea of placing the State, in a separate and unconnected point of view, and the idea of making a transfer of the powers of the general government, are not sufficiently clear or cogent to supercede such momentous considerations.

Having thus, generally, explained the principles contained in my letter of the 5th instant, permit me (without adverting to the material change that has since occurred in the state of our information, relatively to the riots ; and which is calculated to produce a corresponding change of sentiments and conduct) to remark, that many of the facts, that are mentioned by the Secretary of State, in order to shew that the Judiciary Authority of the Union after a fair and full experiment, had proved incompetent to enforce obedience, or to punish infractions of the laws, were, before that communication, totally unknown to me. But still if it shall not be deemed a deviation from the restriction that I have determined to impose upon my correspondence, I would offer some doubts which in that respect, occurred to my mind on the evidence, as it appeared at the time of our conference.—— When I found, that the Marshal had, without molestation, executed his Office in the County of Fayette ;— that he was never insulted or opposed, till he acted in company with General Neville ; and that the virulence of the rioters was directly manifested against the person and property of the latter gentleman, and only incidentally against the person of the former, I thought there was ground yet to suppose (and as long as it was reasonable I wished to suppose) that a spirit of opposition to the officers employed under the Excise law, and not a spirit of opposition to the officers employed in the administration of justice, was the immediate source of the outrages which we deprecate. It is true that these sources of opposition are equally reprehensible ; and that their effects are alike unlawful ; but on a question respecting the power of the Judiciary authority to enforce obedience, or to punish infractions of the law, it seemed to be material to discriminate between the cases alluded to, and to ascertain with precision, the motives and the object of the rioters. Again :—As the Associate Judge had not, at that time, issued his certificate, it was proper to scrutinize, with strict attention, the nature of the evidence, on which an act of Government was to be founded. The Constitution of the Union, as well as of the State, had cautiously provided even in the case of an individual, that " no warrant should

iffue, but upon probable caufe, fupported by oath or affirmation, and particularly defcribing the place to be fearched,
and the perfons or things to be feized." And a much higher
degree of caution might reafonably be exercifed in a cafe, that
involved a numerous body of citizens in the imputation of
treafon, or felony, and required a fubftitution of the military
for the judicial inftruments of coercion. The only affidavits
that I recollect to have appeared at the time of our conference, were thofe containing the hearfay of Col. Mentges,
and the vague narrative of the Poft Rider. The letters that
had been received from a variety of refpectable citizens, not
being written under the fanction of an oath or affirmation,
could not acquire the legal force and validity of evidence,
from a mere authentication of the fignatures of the refpective
writers. Under fuch circumftances, doubts arofe, not whether the means which the laws prefcribe for effectuating their
own execution, fhould be exerted, but whether the exiftence
of a fpecific cafe, to which fpecific means of redrefs were ap-
propriated by the laws, had been legally eftablifhed ;—not
whether the laws, the conftitution, the government, the
principles of focial order, and the bulwarks of private right
and fecurity fhould be facrificed ; but whether the plan propofed, was the beft calculated to preferve thofe ineftimable
bleffings : And, recollecting a declaration, which was made
in your prefence, " that it would not be enough for a military force to difperfe the infurgents, and to reftore matters to
the fituation in which they were, two or three weeks before
the riots were committed, but that the force muft be continued for the purpofe of protecting the officers of the revenue and fecuring a perfect acquiefcence in the obnoxious
law," I confefs, fir, the motives to caution and deliberation
ftrike my mind with accumulated force. I hope, however,
that it will never ferioufly be contended, that a military force
ought now to be raifed with any view, but to fupprefs the
rioters ; or that if raifed with that view, it ought to be em-

ployed for any other. The difperfion of the infurgents is, indeed, obvioufly the fole objeƈt for which the aƈt of Congrefs has authorized the ufe of military force, on occafions like the prefent ; for with a generous and laudable precaution, it exprefsly provides that even before that force may be called forth, a proclamation fhall be iffued, commanding the infur-gents to difperfe, and retire peaceably to their refpeƈtive abodes, within a limited time.

But the force of thefe topics I again refer implicitly to your decifion ; convinced, Sir, that the goodnefs of your intentions, now, not lefs than heretofore, merits an affeƈtionate fupport from every defcription of your fellow citizens. For my own part, I derive a confidence from the heartfelt integrity of my views, the fincerity of my profeffions, which renders, me invulnerable by any infinuation of praƈtifing a finifter or deceitful policy.

I pretend not to infallibility in the exercife of my private judgment, or in the difcharge of my public funƈtions ; but in the ardour of my attachment, and in the fidelity of my fervices, to our common country, I feel no limitation : And your excellency, therefore, may juftly be affured, that in every way which the conftitution of the United States, and of Pennfylvania fhall authorize and prefent, or future exigencies may require, you will receive my moft cordial aid and fupport.

I am with perfeƈt refpeƈt, Sir
Your Excellency's
Moft obedient humble fervant,
THOMAS MIFFLIN.

Philadelphia, Auguft 12, 1794.

To the Prefident
of the United States.

Communication from the Secretary of State to Governor Mifflin, in answer to his of 12th August to the President of the United States.

Philadelphia, Auguſt 30th, 1794.

Sir,

I AM directed by the Preſident to acknowledge the receipt on the 17th of your Excellency's letter dated the 12th inſtant.

The Preſident feels with you the force of the motives which render undeſirable an extenſion of correſpondence on the ſubject in queſtion. But the caſe being truly one of great importance and delicacy theſe motives muſt yield, in a degree, to the propriety and utility of giving preciſion to every part of the tranſaction, and guarding effectually againſt ultimate miſapprehenſion.

To this end it is deemed adviſeable, in the firſt place, to ſtate ſome facts which either do not appear, or are conceived not to have aſſumed an accurate ſhape in your Excellency's letter. They are theſe.

1. You were informed at the conference, that all the information which had been received had been laid before an aſſociate Juſtice, in order that he might conſider and determine whether ſuch a caſe as is contemplated by the ſecond ſection of the act, which provides for calling forth the militia to execute the Laws of the Union, ſuppreſs inſurrections, and repel invaſions, had occured ; that is, whether combinations exiſted too powerful to be ſuppreſſed by the ordinary courſe of judicial proceedings, or by the powers veſted in the Marſhal by that act—in which caſe, the Preſident is authorized to call forth the militia to ſuppreſs the combinations and to cauſe the laws to be duly executed.

2. The idea of a preliminary proceeding by you was pointed to an eventual co-operation with the Executive of the United States, in ſuch plan as upon mature deliberation ſhould be deemed adviſeable in conformity with the Laws of the Union. The inquiry was particularly directed towards the poſſibility of ſome

previous acceffory ftep in relation to the militia, to expedite the calling them forth if an acceleration fhould be judged expedient and proper, and if any delay on the score of evidence fhould attend the notification from a Judge, which the laws make the condition of the power of the Prefident to require the aid of the militia, and turned more efpecially upon the point, whether the law of Pennfylvania of the 22d of September 1783, was or was not ftill in force. The queftion emphatically was, Has the Executive of Pennfylvania power to put the militia in motion, previous to a requifition from the Prefident under the laws of the Union, if it fhall be thought advifeable fo to do ? Indeed it feems to be admitted by one part of your letter, that the *preliminary* meafure contemplated did turn on this queftion, and with a particular eye to the authority and exiftence of the act juft mentioned.

3. The information contained in the papers read at the conference, befides the violence offered to the Marfhal, while in company with the Infpector of the Revenue, eftablifhed, that the Marfhal had been afterwards made prifoner by the Infurgents, put in jeopardy of his life—had been obliged to obtain fafety and liberty by a promife guaranteed by Colonel Prefley Neville, that he would ferve no other procefs on the weft fide of the Alleghany Mountain—that in addition to this; a deputation of the Infurgents had gone to Pittfburgh to demand of the Marfhal a furrender of the proceffes in his poffeffion, under the intimation that it would fatisfy the people *and add to his fafety*; which neceffarily implied that he would be in danger of further violence without fuch a furrender. That under the influence of this menace he had found it neceffary to feek fecurity by taking fecretly and in the night a circuitous route :

This recapitulation is not made to invalidate the explanation offered in your laft letter of the view of the fubject, which you affert to have led to the fuggeftions contained in your firft, and of the fenfe which you wifh to be received as that of the obfervations accompanying thofe fuggeftions. It is intended folely to manifeſt, that it was natural for the Preſident to regard your communication of the 5th inſtant in the light under which it is preſented in the reply to it.

For, having informed you that the matter was before an aſſociate juſtice, with a view to the law of the United States which has been mentioned, and having pointed what was ſaid reſpecting a *preliminary* proceeding on your part to a call of the militia under the authority of a ſtate law, by anticipation of a requiſition from the General Government and in co-operation with an eventual plan to be founded upon the Laws of the Union. It was not natural to expect, that you would have preſented a plan of conduct entirely on the baſis of the State Government even to the extent of reſorting to the Legiſlature of Pennſylvania, after its Judiciary had proved incompetent, " to preſcribe by their wiſdom and authority the means of ſubduing the ſpirit of inſurrection and of reſtoring tranquility and order ;" a plan, which being incompatible with the courſe marked out in the Laws of the United States, evidently could not have been acceded to without a ſuſpenſion, for a long and indefinite period, of the movements of the Fœderal Executive purſuant to thoſe laws. The repugnancy and incompatibility of the two modes of proceeding at the ſame time cannot it is preſumed be made a queſtion.

Was it extraordinary then, that the plan ſuggeſted ſhould have been unexpected, and that it ſhould even have been thought liable to the obſervation of having contemplated Pennſylvania in a light too ſeparate and unconnected ?

The propriety of the remark, that " it was impoſſible not to think that the current of the obſervations in your letter might be conſtrued to imply a virtual diſapprobation of that plan of conduct on the part of the general government, in the actual ſtage of its affairs, which you acknowledged would be proper on the part of the government of Pennſylvania, if arrived at a ſimilar ſtage," muſt be referred to the general tenor and complexion of thoſe obſervations, and to the inference they were naturally cal-

M

culated to inculcate. If this inference was, that under the known circumstances of the case, the employment of force to suppress the insurrection was improper, without a long train of preparatory expedients—and if in fact, the government of the United States (which has not been controverted) was at that point, where it was admitted that the government of Pennsylvania being arrived, the resort to force on its part would be proper—the impression which was made could not have been effaced by the consideration, that the forms of referring what concerned the government of the Union to the judgment of its own executive were carefully observed. There was no difficulty in reconciling the intimation of an opinion unfavorable to a particular course of proceeding, with an explicit reference of the subject officially speaking to the judgment of the officer charged by the constitution to decide, and with a sincere recognition of the subjection of the individual authority of the state to the national jurisdiction of the Union.

The disavowal by your excellency of an intention to sanction the inference which was drawn, renders what has been said a mere explanation of the cause of that inference and of the impression which it *at first* made.

It would be foreign to the object of this letter to discuss the various observations which have been adduced to obviate a misapprehension of your views, and to maintain the propriety of the course pursued in your first communication. It is far more pleasing to the President to understand you in the sense you desire, and to conclude, that no opinion has been indicated by you inconsistent with that which he has entertained of the state of things, and of his duty in relation to it. And he remarks with satisfaction the effect which subsequent information is supposed calculated to produce favoring an approximation of sentiments.

But there are a few miscellaneous points, which, more effectually to prevent misconception any where, seem to demand a cursory notice.

You obferve that the Prefident had *already determined* to exercife his legal powers in drafting a competent force of the militia.
At the point of time to which you are underftood to refer, namely, that of the conference, the Prefident *had no legal power* to
call forth the militia.   No judge had yet pronounced, that a cafe
juftifying the exercife of that power exifted.   You muft be fen-
fible, fir, that all idea of your calling out the militia by your authority was referred to a ftate of things antecedent to the lawful
capacity of the Prefident to do it by his own authority ; and
when he had once determined upon the call purfuant to his legal
powers, it were abfurd to have propofed to you a feparate and
unconnected call.   How too it might be afked, could fuch a determination, if it had been made and was known to you have
comported with the plan fuggefted in your letter, which prefup-
pofes that the employment of force had not already been determined upon ?

This paffage of your letter is therefore conftrued to mean only,
that the Prefident had manifefted an opinion predicated upon the
event of fuch a notification from a Judge as the law prefcribes,
that the nature of the cafe was fuch as would probably require
the employment of force.   You will alfo, it is believed, recollect
that he had not at the time finally determined upon any thing.—
and that the conference ended with referring the whole fubject to
further confideration.

You fay, that if you had undertaken not only to comply
promptly with the Prefident's requifition, but to embody a diftinct corps for the fame fervice, an ufelefs expenfe would have been
incurred by the ftate, an unneceffary burthen would have been
impofed on the citizens, and embarraffment and confufion would
probably have been introduced inftead of fyftem and co-operation.
But both were never expected.   Your embodying the militia independent of a requifition from the Prefident was never thought of,
except as a preliminary and auxiliary ftep.   Had it taken place
when the requifition came, the corps embodied would have been

ready towards a compliance with it, and no one of the inconveniences suggested could possibly have arisen.

You say, in another place, that you "was *called upon to act* not in conformity to a positive law, but in compliance with the duty which is supposed to result from the nature and constitution of the executive office." It is conceived that it would have been more correct to have said " you was called upon *to be consulted* whether you had power in the given case to call forth the militia, without a previous requisition from the general government." The supposition that you might possess this power was referred to a law of Pennsylvania, which appeared on examination to have been repealed. A gentleman who accompanied you thought that the power, after a due notification of the incompetency of the Judiciary, might be deduced from the nature and constitution of the executive office.

It has appeared to your Excellency fit and expedient to animadvert upon the nature of the evidence produced at the conference and to express some doubts which had occurred to your mind concerning it.

As the laws of the United States have referred the evidence in such cases to the judgment of a District Judge or Associate Justice ; and foreseeing that circumstances so peculiar might arise as to render rules relating to the ordinary and peaceable state of society inapplicable, have forborne to prescribe any ; leaving it to the understanding and conscience of the Judge ; upon his responsibility, to pronounce what kind and degree of evidence should suffice. The President would not sanction a discussion of the standard or measure, by which evidence in those cases ought to be governed. He would restrain himself by the reflection, that this appertains to the province of another, and that he might rely as a guide, upon the decision which should be made by the proper organ of the laws for that purpose.

But it may be no deviation from this rule to notice to you,

that the facts stated in the beginning of this letter under the third head appear to have been overlooked in your survey of the evidence, while they seem to be far from immaterial to a just estimate of it.

You remark that " when you found that the Marshal had without molestation executed his office in the county of Fayette—that he was never insulted or opposed 'till he acted in company with General Neville, and that the virulence of the rioters was directly manifested against the person and property of the latter gentleman and only incidentally against the person of the former. You thought there was ground yet to suppose that a spirit of opposition to the officers employed under the Excise law, *and not a spirit of opposition to the Officers employed in the administration of Justice,* was the immediate source of the outrages which are deprecated.

It is natural to enquire how this supposition could consist with the additional facts which appeared by the same evidence, namely, that the Marshal having been afterwards made prisoner by the rioters had been compelled, for obtaining safety and liberty, to promise to execute no more processes within the discontented scene ; and that subsequently again to this, in consequence of a deputation of the rioters deliberately sent to demand a surrender of the processes in his possession enforced by a threat, he had found it necessary to seek security in withdrawing by a secret and circuitous route—did not these circumstances unequivocally denote, that Officers *employed in the administration of Justice* were as much objects of opposition as those employed in the execution of the particular laws ? And that the rioters were at least consistent in their plan.

It must needs be that these facts escaped your Excellency's attention ; else they are too material to have been omitted in your review of the evidence and too conclusive not to have set aside the supposition which you entertained—and which seems to have had so great a share in your general view of the subject.

There remains only one point on which your Excellency will be longer detained—a point indeed of great importance, and confequently demands ferious and careful reflection. It is the opinion you fo emphatically exprefs, that the mere *difperfion* of the infurgents is the fole object for which the militia can be lawfully called out, or kept in fervice after they may have been called out.

The Prefident referves to the laft moment the confideration and decifion of this point.

But there are arguments weighing heavily againft the opinion you have expreffed which in the mean time are offered to your candid confideration.

The Conftitution of the United States (article 1. fec. 8.) empowers Congrefs " to provide for calling forth the militia to execute the Laws of the Union, fupprefs infurrections and repel invafions" evidently from the wording and diftribution of the fentence contemplating the execution of the Laws of the Union as a thing diftinct from the fuppreffion of infurrections.

The act of May 2d. 1792, for carrying this provifion of the Conftitution into effect adopts for it's title the very words of the Conftitution, being " An act to provide for calling forth the militia to execute the Laws of the Union, fupprefs infurrections and repel invafions," continuing the conftitutional diftinction.

The firft fection of the act provides for the cafes of invafion and of infurrection, confining the latter to the cafe of infurrection againft the Government of a State. The fecond fection provides for the cafe of the execution of the laws being obftructed by combinations too powerful to be fuppreffed by the ordinary courfe of judicial proceedings or by the powers vefted in the Marfhals.

The words are thefe " Whenever the Laws of the United States fhall be oppofed or the execution thereof obftructed in any State by combinations too powerful to be fuppreffed by the ordinary courfe of judicial proceedings or by the powers vefted in the

Marfhals by this act, the fame being notified to the Prefident of the United States by an Affociate Juftice or the Diftrict Judge, it fhall be lawful for the Prefident of the United States to call forth the militia of fuch State *to fupprefs fuch combinations and to caufe the Laws to be duly executed."* Then follows a provifion for calling forth the militia of other States.

The terms of this fection appear to contemplate and defcribe fomething that may be lefs than infurrection. " The combinations" mentioned may indeed amount to infurrections, but it is conceivable that they may ftop at affociations not to comply with the law, fupported by riots, affaffinations and murders, and by a general fpirit in a part of the community which may baffle the ordinary judiciary means with no other aid than the Poffe Comitatus, and may even require the ftationing of military force for a time to awe the fpirit of riot and countenance the magiftrates and officers in the execution of their duty. And the objects for which the militia are to be called are exprefsly *not only* to fupprefs thefe combinations (whether amounting to infurrections or not, *but to caufe the Laws to be duly executed.*

It is therefore plainly contrary to the manifeft general intent of the Conftitution and of this act and to the pofitive and exprefs terms of toe 2d fection of the act to fay that the militia called forth are not to be continued in fervice for the purpofe of *caufing the Laws to be duly executed*, and of courfe 'till they are fo executed.

What is the main and ultimate object of calling forth the militia ? " *To caufe the Laws to be duly executed.*" Which are the laws to be executed ? Thofe which are oppofed and obftructed in their execution by the combinations defcribed in the prefent cafe, the laws laying duties upon fpirits diftilled within the United States and upon ftills—and incidentally thofe which uphold the judiciary functions. When are the laws executed ? clearly when the oppofition is fubdued—when penalties for difobedience can be enforced—when a compliance is effectuated.

Would the mere *difperfion* of infurgents and their retiring to their refpective homes do this? would it fatisfy either member of the provifion, the fuppreffion of the combinations, or the execution of the laws? Might not the former, notwithftanding the *difperfion,* continue in full rigour, ready at any moment to break out into new acts of refiftance to the laws? Are the militia to be kept perpetually marching and countermarching, towards the infurgents while they are embodied and from them when they have feparated and retired?. Suppofe the infurgents hardy enough to wait the experiment of a battle, are vanquifhed and then difperfe and retire home, are the militia immediately to retire alfo to give them an opportunity to reaffemble recruit and prepare for another battle? And is this to go on and be repeated without limit?

Such a conftruction of the law, if true, were certainly a very unfortunate one, rendering its provifions effentially nugatory, and leading to endlefs expenfe and as endlefs difappointment. It could hardly be advifeable to vex the militia by marching them to a diftant point where they might fcarcely be arrived before it would be legally neceffary for them to return, not in confequence of having effected their object—of having " caufed the Laws to be executed" but in confequence of the mere ftratagem of a deceitful difperfion and retiring.

Thus far the fpirit as well as the pofitive letter of the Law combats the conftruction which you have adopted. It remains to fee if there be any other part of it which compels to a renunciation both of the letter and fpirit of the antecedent provifions.

The part which feems to be relied upon for this effect is the third fection, which by way of provifo enjoins " That whenever it may be neceffary in the judgment of the Prefident to *ufe* the military force by that act directed to be called forth he fhall forthwith and previous thereto, by Proclamation, command the Infurgents to difperfe and retire peaceably to their refpective abodes within a limited time." But does this affirm, does it even neceffarily imply, that the militia after the difperfion and retiring, are not to be ufed for the purpofe for which they are authorized to be called forth ; that is " to caufe the laws to be duly executed," to countenance by their prefence, and in cafe of further refiftance to protect and fupport by their ftrength, the refpective civil officers in the execution of their feveral duties whether for bringing delinquents to punifhment, or otherwife for giving effect to the Laws? May not the injunction of this fection be regarded as a merely humane and prudent precaution, to diftinguifh previous to the *actual application* of force a hafty tumult from a deliberate infurrection? to give an opportunity for thofe who may be accidentally or inadvertently mingled in a tumult or diforderly rifing to feparate and withdraw from thofe who are defignedly and deliberately actors? to prevent, if poffible, bloodfhed in a conflict of arms, and if this cannot be done to render the neceffity of it palpable, by a premonition to the infurgents to difperfe and go home? And are not all thefe objects compatible with the further employment of the militia for the ulterior purpofe of caufing the laws to be executed, in the way which has been mentioned? If they prefent a rational end for the provifo, without defeating the main defign of the antecedent provifion, it is clear they ought to limit the fenfe of the former and exclude a conftruction which muft make the principal provifion nugatory.

Do not the rules of law and reafon unite in declaring that the different parts of a ftatute fhall be fo conftrued as if poffible to confift with each other—that a PROVISO ought not to be underftood or allowed to operate in a fenfe tending to defeat the principal claufe ; and that an implication (if indeed there be any fuch implication as is fuppofed in the prefent cafe) ought not to overrule an exprefs provifion—efpecially at the facrifice of the *manifeft general intent* of a law, which in the prefent cafe undoubtedly is, that the Militia fhall be called forth " *to caufe the laws to be duly executed ?*"

Though not very material to the merit of the argument, it may

N

be remarked, that the proviso which forms the 3d section contemplates merely the cafe of infurrection. If the *combinations* described in the 2d section may be less than infurrection, then the proviso is not commenfurate with the whole cafe contained in the 2d section, which would be an additional circumstance to prove that it cannot work an effect which shall be a substitute for the main purpose of the first section.

1 have the honour to be, with perfect respect, Sir, your Excellency's most obedient Servant,

EDM. RANDOLPH.

True Copy.
GEO. TAYLOR, JUN.

Report of the Secretary of the Treasury to the President of the United States, relative to the inexecution of the Excise Law in certain Counties of Pennsylvania.

TREASURY DEPARTMENT, *August 5th,* 1794.

SIR,

THE difagreeable crifis at which matters have lately arrived in fome of the Weſtern Counties of Pennſylvania, with regard to the laws laying duties on Spirits diſtilled within the United States, and on Stills, feems to render proper a review of the circumſtances which have attended thoſe laws in that fcene, from their commencement to the prefent time, and ef the conduct which has hitherto been obferved on the part of the government, its motives and effect—In order to a better judgment of the meafures neceſſary to be purſued in the exiſting emergency.

The oppoſition to thoſe laws in the four moſt Weſtern Counties of Pennſylvania, (Allegheny, Waſhington, Fayette, and Weſtmoreland) commenced as early as they were known to have been paſſed. It has continued, with different degrees of violence, in the different counties, and at different periods—But Waſhington has uniformly diſtinguiſhed its refiſtance by a more exceſſive ſpirit, than has appeared in the other counties, and feems to have been chiefly inſtrumental in kindling and keeping alive the flame.

The oppoſition firſt manifeſted itſelf in the milder ſhape of the circulation of opinions unfavorable to the law, and calculated, by the influence of public difeſteem, to difcourage the accepting or holding of offices under it, or the complying with it, by thoſe, who might be fo difpofed; to which was added the ſhew of a difcontinuance of the bufinefs of diſtilling.

Thefe expedients were ſhortly after fucceeded by private aſſociations to *forbear* compliances with the law. But it was not long before thefe mere negative modes of oppoſition were perceived to be likely to prove ineffectual. And in proportion as this was the cafe, and as the means of introducing the laws into operation were put into execution, the difpofition to refiftance became more turbulent and more inclined to adopt and practife violent expedients. The officers now began to experience marks of contempt and infult. Threats againft them became frequent and loud; and after fome time thefe threats were ripened into acts of ill treatment and outrage.

Thefe acts of violence were preceded by certain meetings of malcontent perfons, who entered into refolutions calculated at once to confirm, enflame, and fyftematize the fpirit of oppofition.

The firft of thefe meetings was holden at a place called Red-Stone Old Fort, on the 27th of July, 1791, where it was concerted that county committees fhould be convened in the four counties, at the refpective feats of juftice therein. On the 23d of Auguft following, one of thefe committees affembled in the county of Wafhington.

This meeting paffed fome intemperate refolutions which were afterwards printed in the Pittfburgh Gazette, containing a ftrong cenfure on the law, declaring that any perfon *who had accepted or might accept an office under Congrefs in order to carry it into effect, fhould be confidered as inimical to the interefts of the Country; and recommending to the Citizens of Wafhington County to treat every perfon who had accepted or might thereafter accept any fuch Office with contempt, and abfolutely to refufe all kind of communication or intercourfe with the Officers, and to withhold from them all aid, fupport, or comfort.*

Not content with this vindictive profcription of thofe who might efteem it their duty, in the capacity of Officers, to aid in the execution of the conftitutional laws of the land, the meeting proceeded to accumulate topics of crimination of the government, though foreign to each other; authorizing by this zeal for cenfure, a fufpicion that they were actuated, not merely by the diflike of a particular law, but by a difpofition to render the government itfelf unpopular and odious.

This meeting, in further profecution of their plan, deputed three of their members to meet delegates from the counties of Weftmoreland, Fayette, and Alleghany on the firft Tuefday of September following, for the purpofe of expreffing the fenfe of the people of thofe counties in an addrefs to the Legiflature of the United States, upon the fubject of the Excife Law, and *other grievances.*

Another meeting accordingly took place on the 7th of September, 1791, at Pittfburgh, in the county of Alleghany, at which there appeared perfons in character of delegates from the four Weftern counties.

This meeting entered into refolutions more comprehenfive in their objects and not lefs inflammatory in their tendency, than thofe which had before paffed the meeting in Wafhington. Their refolutions contained fevere cenfures not only on the law which was the immediate fubject of objection, but upon what they termed the exorbitant falaries of officers ; the unreafonable intereft of the public debt ; the want of difcrimination between original holders and transferrees, and the inftitution of a National Bank. The fame unfriendly temper towards the government of the United States, which feemed to have led out of their way the meeting at Wafhington appears to have produced a fimilar wandering in that at Pittfburgh.

A reprefentation to Congrefs and a remonftrance to the Legiflature of Penn'ylvania againft the law, more particularly complained of were prepared by this meeting—publifhed together with their other proceedings in the Pittfburgh Gazette, and afterwards prefented to the refpective bodies to whom they were addreffed.

Thefe meetings compofed of very influential individuals, and conducted without moderation or prudence, are juftly chargeable with the exceffes which have been from time to time committed ; ferving to give confiftency to an oppofition which has at length matured to a point, that threatens the foundations of the Government and of the Union—unlefs fpeedily and effectually fubdued.

On the 6th of the fame month of September, the oppofition broke out in an act of violence upon the perfon and property of Robert Johnfon, Collector of the Revenue for the counties of Alleghany and Wafhington.

A party of men armed and difguifed, way laid him at a place on Pigeon Creek in Wafhington county, feized, tarred and feathered him, cut off his hair, and deprived him of his horfe, obliging him to travel on foot a confiderable diftance in that mortifying and painful fituation.

The cafe was brought before the Diftrict Court of Pennfylvania, out of which proceffes iffued againft John Robertfon, John Hamilton, and Thomas M'Comb—three of the perfons concerned in the outrage.

The ferving of thefe proceffes was confided by the then Marfhal Clement Biddle, to his Deputy Jofeph Fox, who in the month of October went into Alleghany county for the purpofe of ferving them.

The appearances and circumftances which Mr. Fox obferved himfelf, in the courfe of his journey, and learnt afterwards upon his arrival at Pittfburgh, had the effect of deterring him from the fervice of the proceffes, and unfortunately led to adopt the injudicious and fruitlefs expedient of fending them to the parties by a private meffenger under cover.

The Deputy's report to the Marfhal, ftates a number of particulars evincing a confiderable fermentation in the part of the country to which he was fent, and inducing a belief on his part, that he could not with fafety have executed the proceffes. The Marfhal tranfmitting this report to the Diftrict Attorney, makes the following obfervations upon it. " I am forry to add that he (the Deputy) found the people in general in the weftern part of this State, and particularly beyond the Alleghany Mountain, in fuch a ferment on account of the act of Congrefs for laying a duty on diftilled fpirits, and fo much oppofed the execution of the faid act, and from a variety of threats to himfelf perfonally, although he took the utmoft precaution to conceal his errand, that he was not only convinced of the impoffibility of ferving the procefs, but that any attempt to effect it would have occafioned the moft violent oppofition from the greater part of the inhabitants, and he declares that if he had attempted it, he believes he fhould not have returned alive.

" I fpared no expenfe nor pains to have the procefs of the court executed, and have not the leaft doubt that my Deputy would have accomplifhed it, if it could have been done."

The reality of the danger to the Deputy was countenanced by the opinion of General Neville, the Infpector of the Revenue ; a man who before had given, and fince has given numerous proofs of a fteady and firm temper ; and what followed is a further confirmation of it.

The perfon who had been fent with the proceffes, was feized, whipped, tarred, and feathered ; and after having his money and horfe taken from him, was blindfolded, and tied in the woods, in which condition he remained for five hours.

Very ferious reflections naturally occurred upon this occafion. It feemed highly probable, from the iffue of the experiment which had been made, that the ordinary courfe of civil procefs would be ineffectual for enforcing the execution of the law, in the fcene, in queftion—and that a perfeverance in this courfe might lead to a ferious concuffion. The law itfelf was ftill in the infancy of its operation, and far from eftablifhed in other important portions of the Union. Prejudices againft it had been induftrioufly diffeminated, mifreprefentations diffufed, mifconceptions foftered. The Legiflature of the United States had not yet organifed the means by which the Executive could come in aid of the Judiciary, when found incompetent to the execution of the laws. If neither of thefe impediments to a decifive exertion had exifted, it was defirable, efpecially in a republican government, to avoid, what is in such cases the ultimate resort, till all the milder means had been tried without success.

Under the united influence of these considerations, it appeared adviseable to forbear urging coercive measures, till the laws had gone into more extensive operation ; till further time for reflection and experience of its operation had served to correct false impressions, and inspire greater moderation ; and till the Legislature had had an opportunity, by a revision of the law, to remove as far as possible objections, and to reinforce the provisions for securing its execution.

Other incidents occurred from time to time, which are further proofs of the very improper temper that prevailed among the inhabitants of the refractory counties.

Mr. Johnson was not the only officer, who about the same period, experienced outrage. Mr. Wells, Collector of the Revenue for Westmoreland and Fayette was also ill treated at Greensburgh and Union Town ; nor were the outrages perpetrated, confined to the officers ; they extended to private citizens, who only dared to shew their respect for the laws of their country.

Some time in October, 1791, an unhappy man of the name of Wilson, a stranger in the county, and manifestly disordered in his intellects, imagining himself to be a Collector of the Revenue, or invested with some trust in relation to it, was so unlucky as to make enquiries concerning the Distillers who had entered their Stills; giving out that he was to travel through the United States, to ascertain and report to Congress the number of Stills, &c. This man was pursued by a party in disguise, taken out of his bed, carried about five miles back to a Smiths' shop, stripped of his cloaths which were afterwards burnt, and after having been himself inhumanly burnt in several places with a heated iron, was tarred and feathered, and about day light dismissed, naked, wounded, and otherwise in a very suffering condition. These particulars are communicated in a letter from the Inspector of the Revenue of the 17th of November, who declares that he had then himfelf feen the unfortunate Maniac, the abufe of whom, as he expreffes it, exceeded defcription, and was fufficient to make human nature fhudder. The affair is the more extraordinary as perfons of weight and confideration in that country are underftood to have been actors in it, and as the fymptoms of infanity were during the whole time of inflicting the punifhment apparent—the unhappy fufferer difplaying the heroic fortitude of a man who conceived himfelf to be a martyr to the difcharge of fome important duty.

Not long after a perfon of the name of Rofeberry underwent the humiliating punifhment of tarring and feathering, with fome aggravations, for having in converfation hazarded the very natural and juft, but unpalatable remark, that the inhabitants of that country could not reafonably expect protection from a Government, whofe laws they fo ftrenuoufly oppofed.

The audacity of the perpetrators of thefe exceffes was fo great, that an armed banditti ventured to feize and carry off two perfons who were witneffes againft the rioters in the cafe of Wilfon, in order to prevent their giving teftimony of the riot to a Court then fitting, or about to fit.

Defigns of perfonal violence againft the Infpector of the Revenue himfelf, to force him to a refignation, were repeatedly attempted to be put in execution by armed parties, but by different circumftances were fruftrated.

In the feffion of Congrefs, which commenced in October 1791, the law laying a duty on diftilled fpirits and ftills, came under the revifion of Congrefs as had been anticipated. By an act paffed May 8th 1792, during that feffion, material alterations were made in it—among thefe, the duty was reduced to a rate fo moderate, as to have filenced complaint on that head—and a new and very favorable alternative, was given to the diftiller, that of paying a monthly, inftead of a yearly rate, according to the capacity of his ftill, with liberty to take a licenfe for the precife term, which

O

he fhould intend to work it, and to renew that licenfe for a farther term or terms.

This amending act, in its progrefs through the Legiflature engaged the particular attention of members, who themfelves were interefted in diftilleries, and of others who reprefented parts of the Country in which the bufinefs of diftilling was extenfively carried on.

Objections were well confidered and great pains taken to obviate all fuch as had the femblance of reafonablenefs.

The effect has in a great meafure correfponded with the views of the Legiflature. Oppofition has fubfided in feveral Diftricts, where it before prevailed, and it was natural to entertain and not eafy to abandon a hope, that the fame thing would by degrees have taken place in the four Weftern counties of this ftate.

But notwithftanding fome flattering appearances at particular junctures, and infinite pains by various expedients to produce the defireable iffue, the hope entertained, has never been realized, and is now at an end, as far as the ordinary means of executing laws are concerned.

The firft law left the number and pofitions of the Offices of Infpection, which were to be eftablifhed in each Diftrict for receiving entries of ftills, to the difcretion of the Supervifor. The fecond, to fecure a due accomodation to diftillers, provides, peremptorily, that there fhall be one in each County.

The idea was immediately embraced, that it was a very important point in the fcheme of oppofition to the law, to prevent the eftablifhment of offices in the refpective counties.

For this purpofe, the intimidation of well-difpofed inhabitants was added to the plan of molefting and obftructing the officers by force or otherwife, as might be neceffary. So effectually was the firft point carried (the certain deftruction of property, and the peril of life being involved) that it became almoft impracticable to obtain fuitable places for Offices in fome of the Counties ;

and when obtained, it was found a matter of neceſſity in almoſt every inſtance to abandon them.

After much effort the Inſpector of the Revenue ſucceeded in procuring the houſe of William Faulkner a Captain in the army, for an office of inſpection in the county of Waſhington. This took place in Auguſt 1792. The office was attended by the Inſpector of the Revenue in perſon, till prevented by the following incidents.

Captain Faulkner being in purſuit of ſome deſerters from the troops, was encountered by a number of people, in the ſame neighbourhood where Mr. Johnſon had been ill treated the preceding year, who reproached him with letting his houſe for an office of inſpection, drew a knife upon him, threatened to ſcalp him, tar and feather him, and reduce his houſe and property to aſhes, if he did not ſolemnly promiſe to prevent the further uſe of his houſe for an office. Captain Faulkner was induced to make the promiſe exacted ; and, in conſequence of the circumſtance, wrote a letter to the Inſpector, dated the 20th of Auguſt countermanding the permiſſion for uſing his houſe ; and the day following gave a public notice in the Pittſburgh Gazette, that the office of inſpection ſhould be no longer kept there.

At the ſame time another engine of oppoſition was in operation. Agreeable to a previous notification, there met at Pittſburgh, on the 21ſt of Auguſt, a number of perſons, ſtiling themſelves " A meeting of ſundry Inhabitants of the Weſtern counties of Pennſylvania."

This meeting entered into reſolutions not leſs exceptionable than thoſe of its predeceſſors. The preamble ſuggeſts that a *tax* on *ſpirituous liquors* is unjuſt in itſelf and oppreſſive upon the poor, that *internal taxes upon conſumption* muſt, in the end deſtroy the liberties of every country in which they are introduced—that the law in queſtion, from certain local circumſtances which are ſpecified would bring immediate diſtreſs and ruin upon the Weſtern country ; and concludes with the ſentiment, that they think it their duty to perfift in remonftrances to Congrefs, and in every other *legal*-meafure that may obftruct the *operation* of the law.

The refolutions then proceed, firft, to appoint a Committee to prepare and caufe to be prefented to Congrefs, an addrefs ftating objections to the law, and praying for its repeal—fecondly to appoint Committees of correfpondence for Wafhington, Fayette and Alleghany, charged to correfpond together, and with fuch committee as fhould be appointed for the fame purpofe in the County of Weftmoreland or with any Committees of a fimilar nature, that might be appointed in other parts of the United States ; and alfo if found neceffary to call together either general meetings of the people in their refpective Counties, or conferences of the feveral Committees ; and laftly to declare that they will in future confider thofe who hold offices for the collection of the duty, as unworthy of their friendfhip, that they will have *no intercourfe nor dealings with them*, will *withdraw* from them *every affiftance, withhold all the comforts of life which depend upon thofe duties, that as men and fellow-citizens we owe to each other, and will upon all occafions treat them with contempt* ; earneftly RECOMMENDING IT TO THE PEOPLE AT LARGE TO FOLLOW THE SAME LINE OF CONDUCT TOWARDS THEM.

The idea of purfuing *legal* meafures to *obftruct* the *operation* of *a law* needs little comment. Legal meafures may be purfued to procure the repeal of a law, but to *obftruct its operation* prefents a contradiction in terms. The *operation* or what is the fame thing the *execution* of a *law* cannot be *obftructed* after it has been conftitutionally enacted, without illegality and crime. The expreffion quoted is one of thofe phrafes, which can only be ufed to conceal a diforderly and culpable intention under forms that may efcape the hold of the law.

Neither was it difficult to perceive, that the anathema pronounced againft the officers of the revenue, placed them in a ftate of virtual outlawry, and operated as a fignal to all thofe who were bold enough to encounter the guilt and the danger to violate both their lives and their properties.

The foregoing proceedings, as foon as known, were reported by the Secretary of the Treafury to the Prefident. The Prefident on the 15th of September, 1792, iffued a proclamation——" earneftly admonifhing and exhorting all perfons whom it might concern to refrain and defift from all unlawful combinations and proceedings whatfoever, having for object or tending to obftruct the operation of the laws aforefaid, inafmuch as all lawful ways and means would be put in execution for bringing to juftice the infractors thereof and fecuring obedience thereto : and moreover, charging and requiring all courts, magiftrates and officers whom it might concern, according to the duties of their feveral offices, to exert the powers in them refpectively vefted by law for the purpofes aforefaid ; thereby alfo enjoining and requiring all perfons whomfoever, as they tendered the welfare of their country, the juft and due authority of Government and the prefervation of the public peace, to be aiding and affifting therein according to law.——And likewife directed, that profecutions might be inftituted againft the offenders, in the cafes in which the laws would fupport and the requifite evidence could be obtained.

Purfuant to thefe inftructions, the Attorney General, in co-operation with the Attorney of the Diftrict attended a Circuit Court, which was holden at York Town in October 1792—for the purpofe of bringing forward profecutions in the proper cafes.

Collateral meafures were taken to procure for this purpofe the neceffary evidence.

The Supervifor of the Revenue was fent into the oppofing furvey—to afcertain the real ftate of that furvey—to obtain evidence of the perfons who were concerned in the riot in Faulkner's cafe, and of thofe who compofed the meeting at Pittfburgh to uphold the confidence and encourage the perfeverance of the officers acting under the law—and to induce if poffible the inhabitants of that part of the furvey, which appeared leaft difinclined to come voluntarily into the law, by arguments addreffed to their fenfe of duty, and exhibiting the eventual dangers and mifchiefsofrefiftance.

The miffion of the fupervifor had no other fruit than that of obtaining evidence of the perfons who compofed the meeting at Pittfburgh, and of two who were underftood to be concerned in the riot—and a confirmation of the enmity which certain active and defigning leaders had induftrioufly infufed into a large proportion of the Inhabitants, not againft the particular laws in queftion only, but of a more ancient date, againft the government of the United States itfelf.

The then Attorney General being of opinion, that it was at beft a doubtful point, whether the proceedings of the meeting at Pittfburgh contained indictable matter, no profecution was attempted againft thofe who compofed it, though if the ground for proceeding againft them had appeared to be firm, it is prefumed, that the trueft policy would have dictated that courfe.

Indictments were preferred to the Circuit Court, and found againft the two perfons underftood to have been concerned in the riot, and the ufual meafures were taken for carrying them into effect.

But it appearing afterwards, from various reprefentations fupported by fatisfactory teftimony, that there had been fome miftake as to the perfons accufed—Juftice and policy demanded that the profecution fhould be difcontinued, which was accordingly done.

This iffue of the bufinefs unavoidably defeated the attempt to eftablifh examples of the punifhment of perfons who engaged in a violent refiftance to the laws—and left the officers to ftruggle againft the ftream of refiftance, without the advantage of fuch examples.

The following plan, afterwards fuccefsfully executed, was about to be digefted, for carrying, if poffible the laws into effect without the neceffity of recurring to force.

1ft To profecute delinquents in the cafes in which it could be clearly done for non compliance with the laws. 2. To intercept the markets for the furplus produce of the diftillers of the non complying counties, by feizing the fpirits in their way to thofe markets, in places where it could be effected without oppofition. 3. By purchafes, through agents, for the ufe of the army (inftead of deriving the fupply through contractors as formerly) confining them to fpirits, in refpect to which there had been a compliance with the laws.

The motives to this plan fpeak for themfelves. It aimed befides the influence of penalties on delinquents, at making it the general intereft of the diftillers. to comply with the laws, by interrupting the Market for a very confiderable furplus, and by, at the fame time, confining the benefit of the large demand for public fervice to thofe who did their duty to the public, and furnifhing through the means of payments in cafh, that medium for paying the duties, the want of which was alledged to be a great difficulty in the way of compliance.

But two circumftances confpired to counteract the fuccefs of the plan—one the neceffity, towards incurring the penalties of non-compliance of there being an office of Infpection in each County, which was prevented in fome of the Counties, by the means of intimidation practifed for that purpofe— another the non-extenfion of the law to the Territory North Weft of the Ohio, into which a large proportion of the furplus beforementioned was fent.

A cure for thefe defects could only come from the Legifature—accordingly in the feffion which began in November

1792, 'meafures were taken for procuring a further revifion of the laws. A bill containing amendments of thofe and other defects was brought in ;—but it fo happened that this object by reafon of more urgent bufinefs, was deferred till towards the clofe of the feffion and finally went off through the ufual hurry of that period.

The continuance of the embarraffment incident to this ftate of things, naturally tended to diminifh much of the efficacy of the plan which had been devifed. Yet it was refolved as far as legal provifions would bear out the Officers, to purfue it with perfeverance; there was ground to entertain hopes of its good effect, and it was certainly the moft likely courfe which could have been adopted towards attaining the object of the laws by means fhort of force ;—evincing unequivocally, the fincere difpofition to avoid this painful refort, and the fteady moderation, which have characterifed the meafures of the Government.

In purfuance of this plan, profecutions were occafionally inftituted in the mildeft forms, feizures were made as opportunities occurred—and purchafes on public account were carried on.

It may be incidently remarked, that thefe purchafes were extended to other places; where, though the fame diforders did not exift, it appeared, advifeable to facilitate the payment of the duties by this fpecies of accommodation.

Nor was this plan, notwithftanding the deficiency of legal provifion, which impeded its full execution, without corref-ponding effects.

Symptoms from time to time appeared which authorifed expectation, that with the aid, at another feffion, of the defired fupplementary provifions, it was capable of accomplifhing its end, if no extraordinary events occurred.

The opponents of the laws, not infenfible of the tendency of that plan, nor of the defects in the laws which interfered with it, did not fail from time to time to purfue analogous modes of counteraction.——The effort to fruftrate the efta-blifhment of offices of infpection, in particular, was perfifted in, and even increafed ; means of intimidating officers and others continued to be exerted.

In April 1793, a party of armed men in difguife, made an attack in the night upon the houfe of a Collector of the reve-nue, who refided in Fayette county; but he happening to be from home, they contented themfelves with breaking open his houfe, threatening, terrifying, and abufing his family.

Warrants were iffued for apprehending fome of the rioters upon this occafion, by Ifaac Mafon, and James Findley Af-fiftant Judges of Fayette county, which were delivered to the Sheriff of that county, who it feems refufed to execute them ;—for which he has fince been indicted.

This is at once an example of a difpofition to fupport the laws of the Union, and of an oppofite one in the local offi-cers of Pennfylvania within the non-complying fcene.

But it is a truth too important not to be noticed and too injurious not to be lamented, that the prevailing fpirit of thofe officers has been either hoftile or lukewarm to the exe-cution of thofe laws—and that the weight of an unfriendly official influence has been one of the moft ferious obftacles, with which they have had to ftruggle.

P

In June following, the Infpector of the Revenue, was burnt in effigy in Alleghany County, at a place, and on a day of fome public election, with much difplay, in the prefence of, and without interruption from Magiftrates and other Public Officers.

On the night of the 22d of November, another party of men, fome of them armed, and all in difguife, went to the houfe of the fame Collector of Fayette, which had been vifited in April, broke and entered it, and demanded a furrender of the Officers Commiffion, and Official Books. Upon his refufing to deliver them up, they prefented piftols at him, and fwore, that if he did not comply, they would inftantly put him to death. At length, a furrender of the Commiffion and Books was enforced. But not content with this, the Rioters, before they departed, required of the Officer, that he fhould within two weeks publifh his refignation on pain of another vifit, and the deftruction of his houfe.

Notwithftanding thefe exceffes the laws appeared during the latter periods, of this year (1793) to be rather gaining ground. Several principal diftillers, who had formerly held out, complied, and others difcovered a difpofition to comply, which was only reftrained by the fear of violence.

But thefe favourable circumftances ferved to beget alarm, among thofe who were determined, at all events, to prevent the quiet eftablifhment of the laws. It foon appeared that they meditated by frefh and greater exceffes to aim a ftill more effectual blow at them ;—to fubdue the growing fpirit of compliance, and to deftroy entirely the organs of the laws, within that part of the Country, by compelling all the Officers to renounce their offices.

The laft proceeding in the cafe of the Collector of Fayette, was in this fpirit. In January of the prefent year, further violences appear to have been perpetrated, William Richmond, who had given information againſt ſome of the Rioters, in the affair of Wilſon, had his barn burnt with all the grain and hay which it contained ; and the ſame thing happened to Robert Shawhan, a Diſtiller, who had been among'the firſt to comply with the law, and who had always ſpoken favorably of it. But in neither of theſe inſtances, (which happened in the County of Alleghany) though the preſumptions were violent, was any poſitive proof obtained.

The Inſpector of the Revenue, in a letter of the 27th of February, writes, that he had received information, that perſons living near the dividing line of Alleghany and Waſhington, had thrown out threats of tarring and feathering one William Cochran, a complying Diſtiller, and of burning his Diſtillery ; and that it had alſo been given out that in three weeks, there would not be a houſe ſtanding in Alleghany County, of any perſon, who had complied with the Laws. In conſequence of which, he had been induced to pay a viſit to ſeveral leading individuals in that quarter, as well to aſcertain the truth of the information, as to endeavour to avert the attempt to execute ſuch threats.

It appeared afterwards, that on his return home, he had been purſued by a collection of diſorderly perſons, threatening as they went along, vengeance againſt him. On their way theſe men called at the houſe of James Kiddoe, who had recently complied with the laws, broke into his Still-houſe, fired ſeveral balls under his ſtill, and ſcattered fire over and about the Houſe.

Letters from the Inſpector, in March, announce an encreaſed activity in promoting oppoſition to the laws—frequent meetings to cement and extend the combinations againſt it ; and among other means for this purpoſe, a plan of collecting a force to feize him, compel him to refign his Commiffion, and detain him prifoner—probably as a hoftage.

In May and June, new violences were committed. James Kiddoe, the perfon above-mentioned, and William Cochran, another complying Diftiller, met with repeated injury to their property. Kiddoe, had parts of his grift-mill, at different times carried away; and Cochran fuffered more material injuries. His Still was deftroyed, his faw-mill was rendered ufelefs, by the taking away of the faw, and his grift-mill fo injured, as to require to be repaired at confiderable expenfe.

At the laft vifit, a note in writing was left requiring him to publifh what he had fuffered, in the Pittfburgh Gazette, on pain of another vifit; in which he is threatened, in figurative, but intelligible terms, with the deftruction of his property by fire. Thus adding to the profligacy of doing wanton injuries to a fellow-citizen, the tyranny of compelling him to be the publifher of his wrongs.

June being the month for receiving annual entries of Stills, endeavours were ufed to open Offices in Weftmoreland and Wafhington, where it had been hitherto found impracticable. With much pains and difficulty, places were procured for the purpofe. That in Weftmoreland, was repeatedly attacked in the night, by armed men, who frequently fired upon it; but according to a report which has been made to this Department, it was defended with fo much courage and perfeverance, by John Wells, an auxiliary officer, and Philip Ragan, the owner of the houfe as to have been maintained during the remainder of the month.

That in Wafhington, after repeated attempts, was fuppreffed. The firft attempt was confined to pulling down the fign of the Office, and threats of future deftruction. The fecond

effected the object in the following mode. About twelve
perſons, armed and painted black, in the night of the 6th of
June, broke into the houſe of John Lynn where the Office
was kept, and after having treacherouſly ſeduced him to come
down ſtairs, and put himſelf in their power, by a promiſe of
ſafety to himſelf and his houſe, they ſeized and tied him,
threatened to hang him, took him to a retired ſpot in the
neighbouring wood ; and there, after cutting off his hair, tarring and feathering him ſwore him never again to allow the
uſe of his houſe for an Office, never to diſcloſe their names,
and never again to have any ſort of agency in aid of the
Exciſe : Having done which, they bound him naked to a
tree, and left him in that ſituation till morning ; when he ſucceeded in extricating himſelf. Not content with this, the
Malcontents ſome days after, made him another viſit ; pulled
down part of his houſe, and put him in a ſituation to be obliged to become an exile from his own home, and to find an
aſylum elſewhere.

During this time, ſeveral of the diſtillers, who had made
entries and benefited by them, refuſed the payment of the
duties ; actuated no doubt by various motives.

Indications of a plan to proceed againſt the Inſpector of the
Revenue, in the manner which has been before mentioned,
continued. In a letter from him of the 10th of July, he
obſerved, that the threatened viſit had not yet been made,
though he had ſtill reaſon to expect it.

In the Seſſion of Congreſs, which began in December 1793,
a bill for making the amendments in the Laws, which had been
for ſome time deſired, was brought in, and on the 5th of June
laſt became a Law.

It is not to be doubted, that the different ſtages of this buſineſs was regularly notified to the Malcontents, and that a con-

viction of the tendency of the amendments contemplated to effectuate the execution of the Law, had matured the refolution to bring matters to a violent crifis.

The encreafing energy of the oppofition, rendered it indifpenfable to meet the evil with proportionable decifion. The idea of giving time for the law to extend itfelf, in fcenes where the difatisfaction with it was the effect, not of an improper fpirit, but of caufes which were of a nature to yield to reafon, reflection, and experience (which had conftantly weighed in the eftimate of the meafures proper to be purfued) had, had its effect, in an extenfive degree. The experiment, too, had been long enough tried, to afcertain, that where refiftance continued, the root of the evil lay deep, and required meafures of greater efficacy, than had been purfued. The laws had undergone repeated revifions of the Legiflative Reprefentatives, of the Union, and had virtually received their repeated fanction, without even an attempt, as far as is now recollected, or can be traced, to effect their repeal ;— affording an evidence of the general fenfe of the community in their favour. Complaints began to be loud, from complying quarters, againft the impropriety, and injuftice of fuffering the laws to remain unexecuted in others.

Under the united influence of thefe confiderations, there was no choice but to try the efficiency of the laws in profecuting with vigour, delinquents, and offenders.

Procefs iffued againft a number of non-complying diftillers in the Counties of Fayette and Alleghany ; and indictments having been found at a Circuit Court holden at Philadelphia in July laft, againft Robert Smilie and John M'Culloch two of the Rioters in the attack, which in November preceeding had been made upon the houfe of a Collector of the Revenue in

Fayette County, proceffes iffued againft them alfo, to bring them to trial; and if guilty to punifhment.

The Marfhal of the Diftrict went in perfon to ferve thefe proceffes. He executed his truft without interruption, though under many difcouraging circumftances, in Fayette County; but while he was in the execution of it in Alleghany County being then accompanied by the Infpector of the Revenue (to wit) on the 15th of July laft he was befet on the road by a party of from thirty to forty armed men, who after much previous irregularity of conduct, finally fired upon him; but as it happened without injury either to him or the Infpector.

This attempt on the Marfhal was but the prelude of greater exceffes.

About break of day, the 16th of July, in conformity with a plan, which feems to have been for fome time entertained, and which probably was only accelerated by the coming of the Marfhal into the Survey, an attack, by about one hundred perfons armed with guns and other weapons, was made upon the houfe of the Infpector in the vicinity of Pittfburgh. The Infpector, tho' alone vigoroufly defended himfelf againft the affailants and obliged them to retreat, without accomplifhing their purpofe.

Apprehending that the bufinefs would not terminate here, he made application by letter to the Judges, Generals of Militia, and Sheriff of the County for protection. A reply to his application, from John Wilkins jun. and John Gibfon Magiftrates and Militia Officers, informed him, that the laws could not be executed, fo as to afford him the protection to which he was entitled, owing to the too general combination of the people in that part of Pennfylvania, to oppofe the Revenue law; adding, that they would take every ftep in their power to bring the Rioters to juftice, and would be glad to receive information of the individuals concerned in the attack upon his houfe, that profecutions might be commenced againft them; and exprefling their forrow that fhould the *Poffe Comitatus* of the County be ordered out in fupport of the Civil Authority, very few could be gotten that were not of the party of the Rioters.

The day following, the Infurgents re-affembled with a confiderable augmentation of numbers, amounting, as has been computed, to at leaft five hundred; and on the 17th of July, renewed their attack upon the houfe of the Infpector; who in the interval had taken the precaution of calling to his aid a fmall detachment from the Garrifon of Fort Pitt, which at the time of the attack, confifted of eleven men, who had been joined by Major Abraham Kirkpatrick, a friend and connection of the Infpector.

There being fcarcely a profpect of effectual defence againft fo large a body as then appeared, and as the Infpector had every thing to apprehend for his perfon, if taken, it was judged advifeable that he fhould withdraw from the houfe to a place of concealment; Major Kirkpatrick generoufly agreeing to remain with the eleven men, in the intention, if practicable to make a capitulation in favour of the property, if not to defend it as long as poffible.

A parley took place under cover of a flag, which was fent by the Infurgents to the houfe to demand, that the Infpector fhould come forth, renounce his office, and ftipulate never again to accept an office under the fame laws. To this it was replied, that the infpector had left the houfe, upon their firft approach, and that the place to which he had retired was unknown. They then declared that they muft have whatever related to his office. They were anfwered that they might fend perfons, not exceeding fix, to fearch the houfe, and take away whatever papers they could find appertaining

to the office. But not satisfied with this they infifted uncon-
ditionally, that the armed men, who were in the houfe, for
its defence, fhould march out and ground their arms, which
Major Kirkpatrick peremptorily refufed ; confidering it, and
reprefenting it to them, as a proof of a defign to deftroy the
property. This refufal put an end to the parley.

A brifk firing then enfued between the Infurgents and thofe
in the houfe, which it is faid lafted for near an hour, till the
affailants having fet fire to the neighboring and adjacent buildings eight in number, the intenfenefs of the heat, and the
danger of an immediate communication of the fire to the
houfe, obliged Major Kirkpatrick and his fmall party to come
out and furrender themfelves. In the courfe of the firing,
one of the infurgents was killed and feveral wounded, and
three of the perfons in the houfe, were alfo wounded. The
perfon killed is underftood to have been the leader of the
party, of the name of James M'Farlane, then a Major in the
militia, formerly a Lieutenant in the Pennfylvania line. The
dwelling houfe, after the furrender, fhared the fate of the
other buildings ; the whole of which, were confumed to
the ground. The lofs of property to the Infpector upon this
occafion, is eftimated, and, as it is believed with great moderation, at not lefs than three thoufand pounds.

The Marfhal, Colonel Prefley Neville, and feveral others
were taken by the Infurgents going to the Infpector's houfe.
All, except the Marfhal and Colonel Neville, foon made their
efcape ; but thefe were carried off fome diftance from the
place where the affray had happened, and detained till one
or two o'clock the next morning. In the courfe of their
detention, the Marfhal in particular fuffered very fevere and
humiliating treatment ; and was frequently in imminent dan-

Q

ger of his life. Several of the party repeatedly prefented their pieces at him, with every appearance of a defign to affaffinate, from which they were with difficulty, reftrained by the efforts of a few more humane, and more prudent.

Nor could he obtain fafety or liberty, but upon the condition of a promife guaranteed by Colonel Neville, that he would ferve no other procefs on the weft fide of the Alleghany mountain. The alternative being immediate death extorted from the Marfhal a compliance with this condition; notwithftanding the juft fenfe of official dignity, and the firmnefs of charaƐter, which were witneffed by his conduƐt throughout the trying fcenes he had experienced.

The infurgents, on the 18th, fent a deputation of two of their number (one a Juftice of the peace) to Pittfburgh, to require of the Marfhal, a furrender of the proceffes in his poffeffion, intimating that his compliance would fatisfy the people, and *add to his fafety;* and alfo to demand of General Neville, in peremptory terms, the refignation of his office, threatning, in cafe of refufal, to attack the place and take him by force: demands which both thefe officers did not hefitate to rejeƐt, as alike incompatible with their honor and their duty.

As it was well afcertained, that no proteƐtion was to be expeƐted from the magiftrates or inhabitants of Pittfburgh, it became neceffary to the fafety, both of the InfpeƐtor and the Marfhal to quit that place; and as it was known that all the ufual routes to Philadelphia were befet by the Infurgents, they concluded to defcend the Ohio, and proceed by a circuitous route, to the feat of government; which they began to put in execution on the night of the 19th of July.

Information has also been received, of a meeting of a considerable number of persons at a place called Mingo Creek Meeting House, in the County of Washington, to consult about the further measures which it might be adviseable to pursue : that at this meeting, a motion was made to approve and agree to support the proceedings which had taken place, until the excise law was repealed, and an act of oblivion passed. But that, instead of this, it had been agreed, that the four Western counties of Pennsylvania and the neighbouring counties of Virginia, should be invited to meet in a Convention of Delegates, on the 14th of the present month at Parkinson's on Mingo Creek, in the county of Washington, to take into consideration the situation of the Western country, and concert such measures as should appear suited to the occasion.

It appears, moreover, that on the 25th of July last the mail of the United States, on the road from Pittsburgh to Philadelphia, was stopped by two armed men, who cut it open, and took out all the letters, except those contained in one packet : these armed men, from all the circumstances which occurred, were manifestly acting on the part of the insurgents.

The declared object of the foregoing proceedings, is to obstruct the execution and compel a repeal of the laws, laying duties on spirits distilled within the United States and upon stills. There is just cause to believe, that this is connected with an indisposition, too general in that quarter, to share in the common burthens of the community; and with a wish, among some persons of influence, to embarrass the government. It is affirmed by well informed persons, to be a fact of notoriety, that the revenue laws of the State itself have always been either refifted or very defectively complied with in the fame quarter.

With the moft perfect refpect, I have the honor to be,
Sir,
Your moft obedient and humble fervant,
(Signed)
ALEXANDER HAMILTON.

To the Prefident
of the United States. }

INSTRUCTIONS TO GOVERNOR LEE.

Bedford, 20th October, 1794.

S i r,

I HAVE it in fpecial inftruction from the Prefident of the United States now at this place, to convey to you on his behalf, the following inftructions for the general direction of your conduct in the command of the militia army, with which you are charged.

The objects for which the militia have been called forth are—

1. To fupprefs the combinations which exift in fome of the weftern counties of Pennfylvania in oppofition to the laws laying duties upon fpirits diftilled within the United States, and upon ftills.

2. To caufe the laws to be executed.

Thefe objects are to be effected in two ways—

1. By military force.

2 By judiciary procefs, and other civil proceedings.

The objects of the military force are twofold.

1. To overcome any armed oppofition which may exift.

2. To countenance and fupport the civil officers in the means of executing the laws.

With a view to the firft of thefe two objects, you will proceed as fpeedily as may be, with the army under your command, into the infurgent counties to attack, and as far as fhall be in your power fubdue, all perfons whom you may find in arms, in oppofition to the laws above mentioned.—You will march your army in two columns, from the places where they are now affembled, by the moft convenient routes, having regard to the nature of the roads, the convenience of fupply, and the facility of co-operation and union; and bearing in mind, that you ought to act, until the contrary fhall be fully developed, on the general principle of having to contend with the whole force of the counties of Fayette, Weftmoreland, Wafhington and Alleghany, and of that part of Bedford which lies weftward of the town of Bedford; and that you are to put as little as poffible to hazard. The approximation, therefore, of your columns, is to be fought, and the fubdivifion of them, fo as to place the parts out of mutual fupporting diftance, to be avoided as far as local circumftances will permit. Parkinfon's Ferry appears to be a proper point, towards which to direct the march of the columns for the purpofe of ulterior meafures.

When arrived within the infurgent country, if an armed oppofition appear, it may be proper to publifh a proclamation, inviting all good citizens, friends of the Conftitution and laws, to join the ftandard of the United States.—If no armed oppofition exift, it may ftill be proper to publifh a proclamation, exhorting to a peaceable and dutiful demeanour, and giving affurances of performing with good faith and liberality, whatfoever may have been promifed by the Commiffioners to thofe who have complied with the conditions prefcribed by them, and who have not forfeited their title by fubfequent mifconduct.

Of thofe perfons in arms, if any, whom you may make prifoners; leaders, including all perfons in command, are to be delivered to the civil magiftrate:—the reft to be difarmed, admonifhed and fent home (except fuch as may have been particularly (violent and also influential) causing their own recognizances for their good behaviour to be taken, in the cases in which it may be deemed expedient.

With a view to the second point, namely, "the countenance and support of the civil officers, in the means of executing the laws," you will make such dispositions as shall appear proper, to countenance and protect, and if necessary and required by them, to support and aid the civil officers in the execution of their respective duties; for bringing offenders and delinquents to justice; for seizing the stills of delinquent distillers, as far as the same shall be deemed eligible by the Supervisor of the Revenue, or chief officer of Inspection; and also for conveying to places of safe custody, such persons as may be apprehended and not admitted to bail.

The objects of judiciary process and other civil proceedings, will be

1. To bring offenders to justice.

2. To enforce penalties on Delinquent Distillers by suit.

3. To enforce the penalty of forfeiture, on the same persons by the seizure of their stills and spirits.

The better to effect these purposes, the Judge of the District, Richard Peters, Esquire; and the Attorney of the District, William Rawle, Esquire, accompany the Army.

You are aware that the Judge cannot be controuled in his functions. But I count on his disposition to co-operate in such a general plan as shall appear to you consistent with the policy of the case. But your method of giving a direction to legal proceedings, according to your general plan, will be by instruction to the District Attorney.

He ought particularly to be inftructed, (with in regard to time and circumftance;) ıft to procure to be arrefted, all influential actors in riots and unlawful affemblies, relating to the infurrection, and combinations to refift the laws ; or having for object to abet that infurrection, and thofe combinations; and who fhall not have complied with the terms offered by the Commiffioners, or manifefted their repentance in fome other way, which you may deem fatisfactory. 2dly. To caufe procefs to iffue for enforcing penalties npon delinqnent Diftillers. 3d. To caufe offenders who may be arrefted, to be conveyed to goals where there will be no danger of refcue—thofe for mifdemeanors, to the goals of York and Lancafter—thofe for capital offences, to the goal of Philadelphia, as more fecure than the others. 4th. To profecute indictable offences in the Courts of the United States—thofe for penalties on delinquents, under the laws before mentioned, in the Courts of Pennfylvania.

As a guide in the cafe, the Diftrict Attorney has with him a lift of the perfons who have availed themfelves of the offers of the Commiffioners on the day appointed.

The feizure of Stills is of the province of the Supervifor and other Officers of Infpection. It is difficult to chalk out a precife line concerning it. There are oppofite confiderations which will require to be nicely balanced, and which muft be judged of by thofe officers on the fpot. It may be found ufeful, to confine the feizures of ftills of the moft leading and refractory Diftillers. It may be advifeable to extend them far in the moft refractory County.

When the infurrection is fubdued, and the requifite means have been put in execution to fecure obedience to the laws, fo as to render it proper for the army to retire (an event which you will accelerate as much as fhall be confiftent with the objet; y..u will endeavour to make an arrangement for detaching such a force as you deem adequate, to be station-ed within the disaffected Country, in such manner as best to afford protection to well-disposed Citizens, and to the Officers of the Revenue, and to repress by their presence, the spirit of riot and oppofition to the laws..

But before you withdraw the army, you will promife on behalf of the Prefident, a general pardon to all such as fhall not have been arrested, with such exceptions as you fhall deem proper. The promife must be fo guarded as not to affect pecuniary claims under the revenue laws. In this meafure, it is advifable there fhould be a co-operation with the Governor of Pennfylvania.

On the return of the army, you will adopt some convenient and certain arrangement for reftoring to the public magazines the arms, accoutrements, military stores, tents and other articles of camp equipage, and entrenching tools which have been furnifhed and fhall not have been confumed or loft..

You are to exert yourfelf by all poffible means to preferve difcipline among the troops, particularly a fcrupulous regard to the rights of perfons and property and a refpect for the authority of the civil Magistrate; taking efpecial care to inculcate and caufe to be obferved this principle, that the duties of the army are confined to the attacking and fubduing of armed opponents of the laws, and to the fupporting and aiding of the civil officers in the execution of their functions..

It has been fettled that the Governor of Pennfylvania will be fecond, the governor of New Jerfey third in command; and that the troops of the feveral States in line, on the march and upon detachment, are to be pofted according to the rule which prevailed in the army during the late war—namely—

R.

in moving towards the fea-board, the mc ▓▓▓▓ treeps will take the right—in moving weftward, the moft northern will take the right.

Thefe general inftructions, however, are to be confidered as liable to fuch alterations and deviations in the detail, as from local and other caufes may be found neceffary the better to effect the main object upon the general principles which have been indicated.

   With great refpect, I have the honor to be,
    Sir,
      Your obedient fervant,
  (Signed)
     ALEXANDER HAMILTON.

Truly copied from the original,

    B. DANDRIDGE.
  Secretary to the Prefident of the United States.